SINGAPORE TO FREEDOM

Copyright

SINGAPORE TO FREEDOM

By

OSWALD W. GILMOUR

DEDICATION

FORWARD

The events and sayings recorded in the following pages are set down entirely from memory, as all records possessed by the author before he left Singapore were lost, and he had neither the materials nor the inclination to make notes on the journey afterwards. He therefore wishes to apologize in advance if he has inadvertently misplaced anyone in the story or incorrectly attributed to anyone any words or actions.

CONTENTS

List of Illustrations

Note on the Current Text

The intention in re-issuing *Singapore to Freedom* (1943) was twofold: first, to ensure the posterity of the text, and second, to make the narrative available to anyone interested in events in South-East Asia during World War II as told from a British perspective.

For an historical contextualization of the events described, the author does a more than adequate job in the first chapters of his narrative and I refer the reader there. As for the story told in these pages, it is a record of an escape from Singapore in 1941 at the time when Japanese troops were moving across South East Asia. On the spine of the original printing it is described as, "The vivid record of a great escape" and turning to the blurb on the inside back cover, one could read:

> *This vivid and authentic story of the author's escape from Singapore just before the island fell describes his gruelling experiences in reaching Ceylon. A first-hand account, it illuminates an aspect of the Malayan tragedy which has yet to receive wide attention. Mr. Gilmour, who was Deputy Municipal Engineer of Singapore, has given us an absorbing narrative of the hazards and hardships of his experience. His book is not one easily abandoned.*

In reproducing the text, I have maintained the original 1943 text almost exactly as it was written. Thus, it includes

iii

some antiquated spellings as well as language and attitudes that will be offensive perhaps to some 21st Century sensibilities.

All the images in the following pages were scanned using the same 1943 hardback first edition as source.

Finally, at the very end of a book, the author included his first attempt at a list of names, addresses/occupations and fates of many of those who attempted the escape at the same time as he did. I am unaware of how much further he progressed in the project and have reproduced the lists as they were printed in the first edition of 1943.

Patrick Gilmour
Brooklyn, NY
November 2020

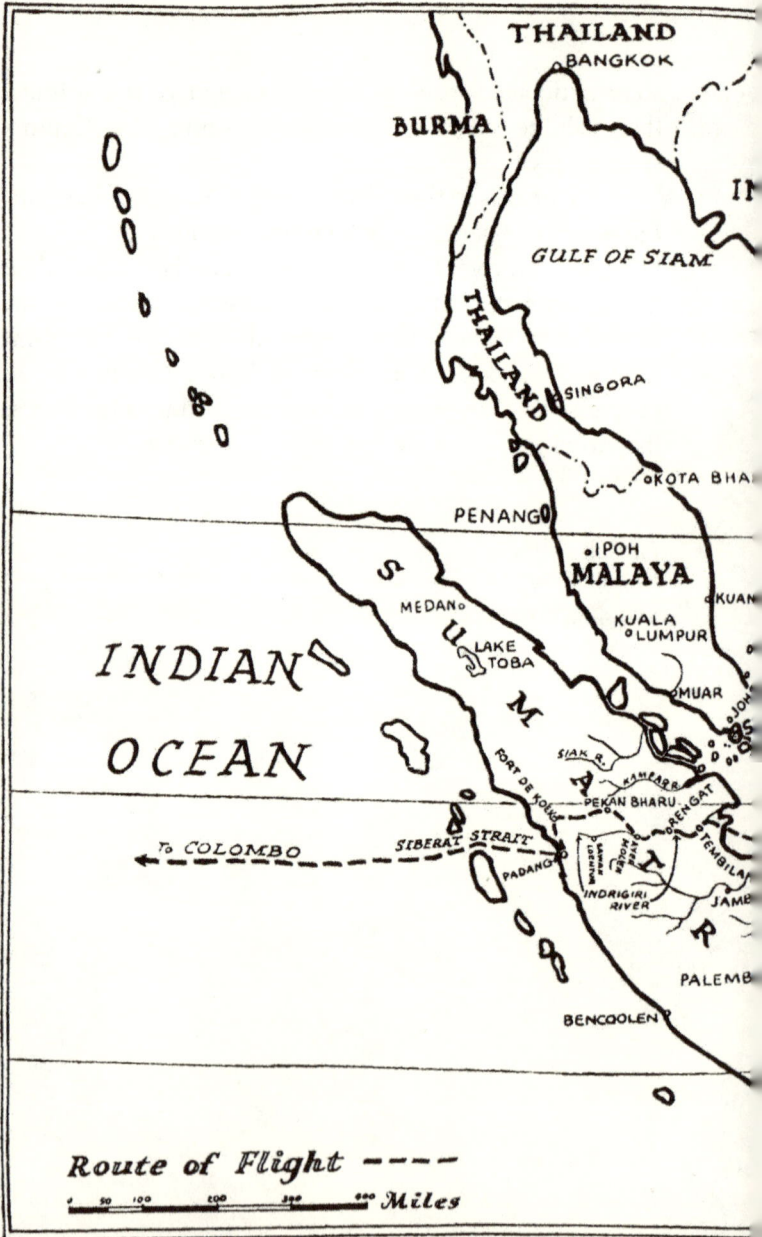

THAILAND
BANGKOK

BURMA

GULF OF SIAM

THAILAND

SINGORA

KOTA BHA

PENANG

IPOH
MALAYA
KUAN

MEDAN
KUALA
LUMPUR

LAKE
TOBA

MUAR

INDIAN

OCEAN

SIAK R.

KAMPAR

FORT DE KOCK

PEKAN BHARU
RENGAT
TEMBILA

To COLOMBO
SIBERAT STRAIT

PADANG
INDRIGIRI
RIVER
JAMB

PALEMB

BENCOOLEN

Route of Flight - - - -
50   100   200   300   400 Miles

Map of South-East Asia and Author's Flight, c.1941

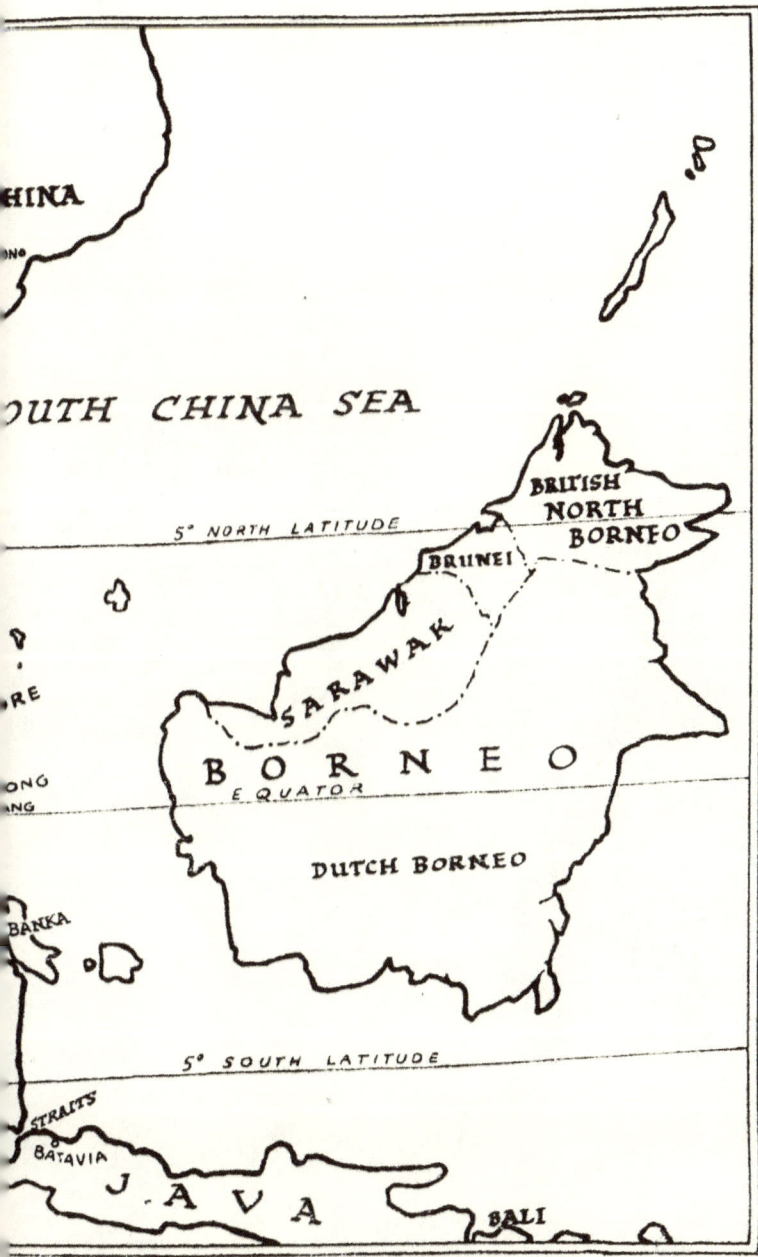

CHINA

SOUTH CHINA SEA

5° NORTH LATITUDE

BRITISH
NORTH
BORNEO

BRUNEI

SARAWAK

B O R N E O

EQUATOR

DUTCH BORNEO

5° SOUTH LATITUDE

STRAITS
BATAVIA
J A V A
BALI

BANKA

CHAPTER ONE

AS WE WERE

IT IS A FAIR GUESS that every present-day schoolboy knows where Singapore is, what it is, and what has happened to it, but when first I passed through the lovely islands at the Western entrance to the harbour in March 1926, Singapore was comparatively unknown even to the adult citizens of the great empire to which it belonged. In the intervening period of nearly sixteen years up to the day when I left it, no town on earth had sunk further from the happiness of obscurity to the misery of world-wide interest. It is also a fair guess to say that, in the second week of February, 1942, Singapore was the most discussed place on the face of the earth. To the residents of Singapore and to others that represented a very undesirable state of affairs.

The resident European civilians of Singapore had been working hard during 1941, but whether that work was to good purpose or not is quite another matter. The Japanese menace had increased almost daily for a long time, and in truly British fashion—at least, we have come to think of it as such—we were trying to do in a short time a great multitude of things which ought to have been done a long time before.

When I say that we, the residents, had been working hard, I do not for a moment wish to make any comparison between the work being done by a European in Singapore and that being done by his brother in Britain during the same period. Such a comparison would be very unfair. Work in Singapore and work in Britain were two very different things. In the former the conditions were unquestionably much more difficult, for Singapore is just a little over one degree north of the equator, and has an average night and day temperature of eighty-seven degrees Fahrenheit, combined with a very high humidity. The slightest exertion of brain or body produced a flow of perspiration which in Malaya was called 'sweat', even in the best circles, because the other word was much too long to be used as often as we wanted to use it. The nights were often so hot that sleep refreshed very little or not at all. In addition to the trials of climate, work was rendered more difficult by a mixture of races with different languages, different mental outlooks, a low average of education, and possibly of intelligence.

The population of Singapore was at that time estimated roughly at about 750,000 people, of whom sixty per cent were Chinese, and the balance made up of Indians and Malays in large numbers, and large sprinklings of many other races, there being about 10,000 Europeans.

During the months preceding the outbreak of war with Japan virtually every Britisher had at least two jobs to do. The younger men under forty-one were doing service— either voluntarily or under compulsion—with one of the Colony's so-called Volunteer Forces, the Malayan Royal Naval Volunteer Reserve, the Straits Settlements Volunteer Force, or the Malayan Volunteer Air Force. The men in the latter two forces would start their ordinary work at seven a.m. or eight a.m. and work through till four-thirty p.m. or five p.m. with perhaps an hour for tiffin. On three or four days a week they would change quickly into uniform after office hours and spend the remaining hours of daylight till seven p.m. in training with their units. The week-ends also were frequently spent in training, or if men were excused from that, their businesses were sure to have a job of work for them on Sunday mornings. For two months each year these men were mobilized completely, and went into camp for intensive training, but even during these periods they were often required to make hasty visits to their offices and to lend a hand when possible with normal duties. The Malayan Royal Naval Volunteer Reserve had been mobilized from the beginning of the war in Europe, and had been doing good work patrolling, mine-sweeping, and manning the signal stations. The men over forty-one were training with the Local Defence Corps—a compulsory service—or were members of a passive defence service such as the Volunteer Police Reserve or the Volunteer Fire Brigade. These duties entailed long hours, often at night, and it frequently came as a surprise to me to find men well advanced in years, with long service in the tropics, standing up to the strain so well as they did. There was a third category for the British European in Singapore: those engaged in essential work who were exempted from service with the fighting forces as they could not be spared from their normal duties, even in an emergency. Often these duties were in the form of a passive defence service also, and required many extra hours of work.

It cannot be said that the Britisher was slack or indifferent about the situation; far from it, he was acutely conscious of his responsibility towards the defence of the Colony and of his duty to the war effort in other spheres.

By the production of rubber and tin Malaya was contributing very essential raw materials, and was, perhaps more than any other part of the Empire, bringing American dollars to the British Treasury. This, before the passing of the Lease-Lend Act, was of paramount importance. To keep the production of these materials flowing along, trade had to be maintained in a thousand ways, and businesses could not be neglected. The tendency in recent years both by public and private enterprises to reduce European staffs put a great deal more responsibility and work on those who were left, and when parts of those staffs were mobilized for training the burden became still greater. The European civilian was working hard in Singapore, beyond question. Faces were strained and men were tired.

Many of the Asiatic community were carrying the burden of the day equally with their European colleagues, and no praise could be too high for the work done by some of them, both then and in the days that followed. There was, however, no compulsory service for the Asiatic, but, in spite of this, many of them were in the Volunteer Forces, and there was also the Malay Regiment, which, I am informed, fought well when called upon to do so. The ranks of the passive defence services were solidly Asiatic, and excellent work they did, under both European and Asiatic officers. It is, nevertheless, primarily of the British European in Singapore that I am speaking.

From the point of view of the United Nations the tragedy in this war has always been that each community has considered that the war would not touch them, and believed that the lot of others would pass them by. Singapore was, undoubtedly, much of the same mind, and while preparations on a large scale were being made, it is still a fact that a great many people thought that these were unnecessary and would never be put to the test.

During 1941, games and entertainments were still being indulged in extensively, and people were comparatively

Western Entrance, Singapore Harbour (Two Views)

Empress Place, Singapore

Government Offices || Town Hall with Fort Canning behind || Municipal Buildings & Cathedral

light-hearted; the hotels and cabarets were usually full, as also were the cinemas. Private house-parties were still numerous, although the scale of the entertainment provided was somewhat reduced. There was no lack of fun and amusement to be had. Singapore had always been devoted to sport, which was officially encouraged as one of the best meeting grounds of the various races contributing largely to the harmony of the cosmopolitan population. The war in Europe had, if anything, increased that devotion as the influx of troops afforded wider competition. On the surface, Singapore would have appeared to the stranger to be normal and to be a fairly gay and wealthy spot. There was no black-out to mar the pleasures of the evening, and no war restrictions on amusements. To the close observer, however, it was noticeable that amusements were being patronized more and more by the fighting services. This was partly due to the increasing numbers of the Services, for each day seemed to bring more and more fighting men to the island; but it was increasingly obvious to residents that the civilian community was, as time went on, seen in less and less numbers at the cinemas, hotels and clubs. The difficulties of war-time business and the demands of war-time service were compelling civilians to use their hours off duty for rest only. This applied to the women as well as the men, for more and more of the former were working at the various War Departments or taking the place of men in business houses. The fighting services had one job only, to be a sailor, soldier or airman, but, as I have said, most of the civilians had two, and spare time with them was not too plentiful.

I counted among my best friends some of the fighting men in Singapore, and so, I think, did most of the civilians; but, like many places where there are large Service establishments, the relations between the Service personnel and the civilians was not always completely happy. The old resident was never entirely reconciled to Singapore being a fortress or to the subordination of civilian interests to Service requirements. It is true that the garrison brought additional trade to the island, but many sighed for the former leisured and universal companionship which seemed to have passed with the coming of the war machine. The Services were accused, among other things, of raising market prices, spoiling servants, and being a little too obvious in clubs and hotels. Small things, of course, but important enough. On the other hand, the Services thought that the civilians lived in conditions of unwarranted luxury, and did not do enough entertaining of the forces in their midst. The standard of living in Singapore was, and always had been, high, but certainly it was not unwarranted. Those who came to Singapore for a few months or a few years were apt to overlook all that a man gave up when he decided to make his life in the tropics. He had, for example, to make a big break with his friends and relatives and face a life in unknown conditions and in a climate which would more than likely shorten his years on this planet. He went to a country where separation from wife and children was the order of the day. Children mostly went home for education at the age of seven or eight, and were only seen by parents for perhaps a few months in all until they reached the late teens or early twenties. A wife frequently found her husband's tour of duty too long for her health, and so came home before he did, and returned after him. All this and other things made it necessary to offer some inducement to men if they were to be persuaded to go to the colonies. This inducement took the form of higher pay and of posts with more responsibility. Men no longer went, if they ever did, to the outposts of the Empire for patriotic motives alone. The great empty spaces of Canada and Australia are testimonies to this. If Britain wants to share the wealth of her colonies, as she undoubtedly does, and if she wants to develop them along the right lines to self-government, she must send well-educated and picked men to these lands, and she must offer something worthwhile to get them. Thus the standard of living in Singapore, while high, was just and necessary.

More might perhaps have been done by civilians to entertain the fighting Services. Much had been done; clubs for these men had been built and run by civilians, entertainments were in most cases available at half price to men in uniform, the existing sporting and social clubs allowed commissioned ranks to join at greatly reduced cost, and many of all ranks were entertained privately. To do more was not so easy as it may have appeared; the civilian population was, as I have said, tired, and often found the strain of entertaining at night too much after their day of office work and war work carried out in tropical heat.

Although the war in Europe had been going on for two years it had not seriously affected the standard of living in Singapore. Most things were still obtainable, many of course at greatly increased prices, for taxes had been raised all round, but only petrol and rice were subject to rationing, and the allowances of these commodities were generous. Cars could not be called a luxury in Singapore, as public transport was not available for more than a small fraction of the community, and it was physically impossible for people to walk long distances in the climate and then carry out their work. The degree of rationing enforced on petrol was about sufficient to cut out joy-riding, but left enough to allow people to get to their offices and do a certain amount of shopping. The rationing on rice cannot have seriously affected the quantities consumed, and was more in the nature of a registration.

Many preparations were being made to meet an emergency. Those of a military nature-which could be seen by anyone-consisted of barbed wire along the whole of the southern waterfront of the island, machine-gun posts in the streets and roads, and the alienation of much land for camps and training-grounds. All types of passive services had been built up and training had been given very generally in Air Raid Precautions, anti-gas measures, and the extinction of incendiary bombs. In a goodly number of cases measures had been taken to protect buildings from bombs, and stocks of food and other essential materials had been created. The people as a whole were confident that if an emergency came to Singapore the island would be ready to meet it, and the news or propaganda released by radio and the Press all tended to increase confidence. We felt that stocks were adequate for a siege, that the defences were powerful, and that the fighting Services, with the possible exception of naval units, were sufficient to meet an attack. When we were told that considerable naval forces, including H.M.S. *Prince of Wales* and H.M.S. *Repulse,* had arrived in Malayan waters, there seemed to be little left to do to ensure the safety of the fortress.

Such, briefly, was the condition of affairs in Singapore on the Saturday when my story really begins.

CHAPTER TWO

A BAD WEEKEND

IT WAS THE MORNING OF SATURDAY, DECEMBER 6th, 1941, and I had arrived in my office in the Municipal Buildings after the usual morning round of engineering works. My job was Deputy Municipal Engineer.

It had been a heavy week, and I was looking forward to an afternoon's rest and a pleasant evening. There was still plenty of work to be done before Monday, but I would do that on Sunday morning, as I have always held that the best time to do hard work in the tropics is the morning-and the earlier the better.

It has always been the custom in hot countries to lie off for an hour or two, when offices are closed, such as on Saturday and Sunday afternoons, and on this particular Saturday I felt I had earned a rest; but, as things turned out, I was not to get it.

Saturday morning from noon to one p.m. was about the busiest hour of the week, and I was hard at it when the telephone rang. A friend of mine, a Colonel in the Sappers, was at the other end. He said he was up against a spot of bother at some Military Works at Krangi, and would like me to have a look at the place and advise him what was best to do. I agreed, and suggested Sunday morning, as the place was some fifteen miles away; but he said that it was very urgent, and would like me to see the site that afternoon. I agreed reluctantly to give up my rest and meet him at two-thirty p.m., which I did. He led me to an area covered with a large number of ammunition stores hidden away among the rubber trees, the existence of which I had not previously known. His problem was the roads which a local contractor had constructed for the military authorities. They were in a frightful state, almost impassable, and the procedure of getting ammunition out and in was laborious and dangerous. It was obvious to me that the roads had never been properly constructed, and that much money had been thrown away on inferior work. I gave him the best advice I could, and departed in a depressed frame of mind. This ammunition dump was certainly of first-class importance, and its usefulness must have been greatly impaired by inexcusable inefficiency. It would take weeks or months to make those roads right, and things were looking pretty grim.

For some time negotiations had been going on between America and Japan, and the outcome of these was likely to seal our fate one way or the other (the Volunteer Forces had already been mobilized for an emergency a week before). In addition, the day's news reported that a large Japanese convoy had been seen in the Gulf of Siam heading westward. I did not know what construction various people put on this news, and still less did I know what the Commander-in-Chief thought about it. To me it meant an attack on Thailand; but still I was not quite happy in that thought, for I could not see any necessity for the Japanese to send a large convoy to invade that country, as the obvious thing was to march in from Indo-China and seize the railway which runs from Bangkok to the border of the two countries. Bangkok, the only port of any importance in Thailand, was difficult or impossible to approach by large ships, whereas the land route, even if the railway was destroyed, was a fairly easy one.

If the C.-in-C. expected an attack on Malaya, then it would appear to a layman that the Fleet, including the newly arrived battleship *Prince of Wales* and cruiser *Repulse,* should have been despatched *immediately* to intercept this convoy before it reached Malayan waters. Aircraft, such as we had, might have been sent to North Malaya to afford protection to the Fleet. This would not have weakened Singapore, for the aircraft could have been brought back at any time in case the attack was directed on Singapore island, and the fixed defences of the island, including some of the largest guns in the world, would have given a good account of themselves in any frontal attack.

After tea, about four-thirty p.m., my wife and I went to the Singapore Cricket Club, hoping to see a rugger game between members of the Services—which was to have been played for charity. We found the game had been cancelled as all the Services had been called back to barracks. Everyone sat around in the club for some time looking glum and wondering if it meant anything. We had had scares before and were getting used to them, but no doubt the situation had deteriorated, as the newspapers say, and we were not so sure that it would blow over this time.

Later, we returned to our house in the Tanglin area, and I spent the rest of the afternoon pottering about my vegetable plots. This matter of growing vegetables was the result of the war, as it was at home. People had been advised by the Government to grow vegetables, but in Malaya it was a very heart-breaking job. It had scarcely been tried before the war, and knowledge on the subject was limited. Almost all soil was bad, and insects played havoc with seeds and plants; still, after much work one could get results, if rather varied, perhaps, in quality. The local vegetables naturally grew better than imported varieties, but in most cases they were not so pleasant eating.

In the evening we had a small dinner-party, but one of our guests could not turn up; he was doing a war job in the evenings at Fort Canning, the Military Headquarters, and that evening he was detained on account of the gravity of the situation. We were all old friends and the party was pleasant enough, but underneath there was a current of apprehension. We went to the Cathay Ballroom to dance after dinner and the town was ominously quiet. As a rule, on Saturday nights the town was full of troops enjoying themselves at the various entertainments and cafes, but on this night they had all disappeared. The ballroom was also quiet, and someone remarked to me that it was a great change to see so few uniforms about.

I found a great deal to do on Sunday morning, but although late for lunch I managed to get a lie-off in the afternoon. We went to church in the evening, and again the atmosphere appeared to be charged with expectant disaster, which reminded me very forcibly of the days before the outbreak of war in Europe, when cars and other noises disappeared from the streets while people were listening to the news broadcasts.

Some visitors dropped in to see us later, and the talk was all of war. They left early and we were in bed shortly after ten o'clock. We had a rude awakening. It must have been the noise which woke us, although our house was about three miles from the centre of the town. The time was approximately 4.10 a.m. I rushed to the verandah of my bedroom, looked towards the town, and I saw searchlights playing in the sky and heard explosions and gunfire. It took quite a few minutes to appreciate what was happening, but the obvious answer was, of course, that an air raid was in progress and, somewhat dazed, I adjusted myself to this thought.

The raid did not last long, but before it had ended I was dressed and ready to go to my Depot. I was in charge of the Rescue, Demolition, Debris and Repair Parties, a passive defence organization entirely manned by members of the Municipal Engineer's staff.

I got to the Headquarters Depot about 4.35 a.m. and tried to contact the A.R.P. Control Room, which should have relayed messages to me asking for assistance if any was required. The Control Room was not working, and I could get no reply. However, after about half an hour I began to get messages from private sources telling me that bombs had fallen in certain places, and that gangs were required to assist in extricating buried persons and clearing the streets. Later, about 5.30 a.m., I think, the Control Room began to function, and the Passive Defence Services got down to work according to plan.

This first raid on Singapore came, of course, without declaration of war, and took most of us by surprise. The streetlights and all ordinary lights which would normally be burning at that hour of the morning were fully lit during this raid. It must, therefore, have been a comparatively easy thing to pick out specific objects even from the height of 17,000 feet, which is said to be the altitude at which the Japanese planes came over.

It is not possible to say exactly what the Japanese were aiming at, but the bombs fell mostly along the banks of the Singapore River; some of them may have been aimed at the Military Head quarters at Fort Canning, or, on the other hand, they may have been dropped indiscriminately by planes following the course of the river from its mouth upwards. In any case, one bomb fell on Guthrie's Building in Battery Road, wrecking the building, and another fell in Raffles Place, near Robinson's new shop, damaging it severely, and this bomb blew out all the windows in the square, which was the main shopping centre. The rest of the bombs fell more or less along the river-banks farther inland on shop houses and go-downs.

About a hundred and forty people were killed in this raid, and a number injured. As the Asiatic population, in many cases, lived very closely packed together, it was natural that a direct hit on a building would result in many casualties. It was not at all uncommon for fifty or more people to be living in one small house, and the house to be flimsy or dilapidated. There were no public shelters and, in the crowded areas, nowhere one could go to obtain any appreciable degree of safety.

When the dawn came that Monday morning I snatched a few seconds between telephone calls to go to the door of my Depot for a breath of air, and I watched the first rays of the sun light up the familiar scene. In the days that followed I was too busy to speculate, but at that moment, perhaps it was a premonition; I thought 'how much longer will I be privileged to witness this'. I was uneasy, but I don't think that, even in those few enlightened seconds, I had any vision of the extent to which the 'Rising Sun' was going to alter my life.

CHAPTER THREE

AT WAR

WAR HAD COME TO SINGAPORE, and the morning paper confirmed this. It told of the widespread nature of Japan's first treacherous attack, the most serious aspect of which, from our point of view, was the landing that had been made in North Malaya. This came to us as a great shock, for we certainly did not expect that the enemy could make a landing on our shores in the course of a few hours.

When the sun rose on December 8th our lives were changed. We knew it, but we never dreamed that the change would be so sudden or so tremendous as it proved to be.

If in any way the residents had neglected their war effort before the Japanese attack they certainly did not do so now. The change which overcame the lives of the people was phenomenal. Sports, games, and parties ceased as though someone had pressed a button. People no longer went to the cinemas nor to the clubs for amusement. A total black-out was immediately enforced, and those who had seen black-out conditions in England and elsewhere said that in Singapore the black-out was one hundred per cent perfect. The streets were empty at nights and little or no traffic was seen except that engaged by the military or on essential services. On moonless nights it was exceedingly difficult to get about, and the number of accidents, mostly to military transport, was very high. Traffic posts in the roads were slaughtered, and the deep roadside drains formed resting-places for innumerable cars and lorries.

The European seldom left his house except for work or war-time service. Neighbours became more neighbourly because the easiest way of obtaining a little social life was to drop into the house next door, as it did not require petrol to get there, and even on the blackest nights it was not hard to find the way. We had always been very friendly with Mr. and Mrs. S. N. Kelly, who lived across the road from us, but during this period we formed the habit of visiting each other for a short time in the evenings if off duty, to discuss the situation, and this, for us, was greatly to affect the shape of things to come.

War makes one live from day to day. People no longer planned ahead or made purchases of anything but consumable stores. Indeed, many Asiatic shops were closed; for, strangely enough, the owners sought safety from bombings by going to up-country towns and villages, either forgetting the threat from the Japanese Army advancing southward, or else they had sufficient faith in the power of our forces to stop the enemy. Some things became difficult to get, especially vegetables, which gave a further stimulus to vegetable growing; but on the whole stocks of food were excellent, and there was no hardship in this direction—except perhaps among some of the coolie class, who had relied on credit systems in certain native shops, and now found those shops closed to them.

Credit had been the blessing and the curse of Singapore. It was pleasant never to be required to carry money about, and to have one's signature accepted anywhere. As this was the case, people seldom bought anything for cash in clubs and hotels; goods of all description were signed for on chits and all shop keepers gave long credits on accounts.

Accounts were rendered monthly, but it cannot be said that they were always paid monthly. After December 8th most shops shut down on the credit system, and this brought about a considerable turnover in people's financial arrangements to meet the situation. Most employers of labour started to pay salaries weekly, or in some cases daily, in contrast to the previous custom of paying all salaries monthly.

Everyone became still more busy for many reasons, the mobilization of the Volunteer Forces had depleted staffs, and the demands of the war had in most cases increased the amount of work which was required to be done. The few European women not yet employed soon had jobs of some sort, and everywhere people were rushing to get things done; no one had a moment to spare.

For a long time men had been prevented from leaving the Colony unless they were unemployed and unemployable or were proceeding on normal transfer or retirement. This step had been taken in order to prevent the depletion of man-power in the Colony during the time when the position with regard to Japanese intentions was uncertain, and of course after the outbreak of war it still held good. There was no restriction on women leaving the Colony, and after the first attack some far-sighted or timorous people sent their wives and children away; as things turned out it would have been very wise to evacuate the women and children right from the beginning. If this had been done a very different tale might have been told.

The face of Singapore itself began to change; certain protective measures had been taken before the war broke out. These measures consisted mostly of building bunds around buildings as a precaution against blast and splinters, and in a few cases air raid shelters had been constructed. In general, however, these elementary precautions had not been taken, and now there was a feverish rush to do the necessary in a very short time. Private people were busy blacking-out their houses and constructing shelters or digging trenches in the garden. The business houses got busy on constructing bunds around all their premises and in removing plate glass windows and substituting boarding for them. All this work by private persons—in addition to the innumerable defence works which were immediately put in hand—caused a shortage of materials, and great ingenuity was necessary to invent means of carrying out work with other than the usual materials. My own Department, which had for months been assisting the Military Authorities and the Government in the construction of many defence works, was called upon to do a vast volume of work. For example, it was required to paint a white line along the centre of every street, to lime-wash the trunks of trees bordering the streets, to remove traffic islands and posts from the roadway, to dig slit trenches in every suitable piece of open ground, to make bridge diversions and to construct aircraft denials on all playing-fields and level grounds. In view of this and the work imposed upon it by the demands of the Rescue and Demolition Organization, all ordinary work of the Department was suspended.

To any city likely to be bombed the Passive Defence Services are of vital importance. Considering the difficulties these services met with in Singapore they were particularly efficient under the test of war. Whatever was lacking was largely due to the reluctance to spend money on equipment and training before the war commenced. When the war had broken out, funds were of course made available in large quantities, but by then it was too late.

When I arrived back in Singapore in July, 1939, after a period of home leave, I found some six months' old correspondence requesting the Municipal Engineer's Department to be responsible for the rescue, demolition, debris, and repair work in case of air raids. I immediately got down to organizing this Service, using the personnel of the Department. My labour force was almost entirely Southern Indian Tamil with a sprinkling of Chinese artisans. The overseers, inspectors, and foremen were Eurasian, Chinese, and Indian. All of these were willing and eager to undertake the work, and it was easy to organize them into suitable parties at three stations in different areas of the town. The question of providing equipment and serviceable shelters at the stations was quite another matter. This involved the expenditure of money, and no one seemed to know where that was to come from. It was a long time before an arrangement was reached between the Government and the Municipal Commissioners as regards expenditure on Passive Defence work. I managed, however, by increasing my stocks of tools for ordinary work, to set some aside in reserve for these rescue parties. After war broke out in Europe we had trial black-outs and Passive Defence exercises at intervals, and my men got to know what would be expected of them in case of raids. Demonstrations were also given and the Passive Defence Services were brought up to a reasonable state of efficiency. My men played at these exercises with enthusiasm, but I was far from satisfied that the organization would be one hundred per cent perfect on the day. There was a lamentable lack of equipment; only a few were provided with steel helmets and gas masks, and there was no uniform whatsoever. The accommodation, tools and plant were quite inadequate, but the greatest lack was capable supervising staff. This was aggravated by the demand of the Volunteer Services.

I myself and most of my European assistants were members of the Volunteer Forces when war broke out in 1939. Some of us were eventually exempted from military service, others were not, and I was never sure what staff I was likely to have when the emergency arose. I always resented this, as it seemed to me to be an uneconomical use of skilled man-power to have Chartered Civil Engineers serving in the ranks of Infantry Volunteer Forces when there was so much important work requiring their skill which was crying out to be done.

A tribunal had been set up by the Government to consider the question of exemptions from military service, and this tribunal was loath to grant exemption except on the strongest grounds. The work which my department was doing had been gazetted as an essential service which had to be carried out in any emergency, so one would naturally expect that the staff would not be taken for military duties. My employers were, however, anxious to release every one they could, and so the staff was split, some going with the Volunteers and some remaining on our essential work. This was, in my opinion, a mistake. I myself, although marked as being exempted 'from continuous training and mobilization', was nevertheless required to train in the evenings during the week why I do not know, it was surely a waste of time. After two years of war I was finally discharged from the Straits Settlements Volunteer Force, being then over forty-one. I had earned a long-service medal with a few years to spare.

When the first raid came I had three stations to operate from, each in charge of one European engineer, and under him were about half-a-dozen more or less reliable Eurasian or Asiatic subordinates, some dozen clerks, and about four hundred men. These stations were at Haveloch Road, Trafalgar Street, and Kallang Road respectively. Haveloch Road was the headquarters, where I took charge.

When I arrived at Haveloch Road at 4.35 a.m. on the 8th December only one clerk had arrived before me, but soon the majority of the staff and labour turned up, and in many cases my squads were first at the incidents. Everything considered, the muster on that first morning did great credit to the men and their training.

All the men worked with a will in clearing-up after this raid. Some people were got out alive from below the debris at Boat Quay and Fisher Street, and clearing proceeded at a reasonable speed. Naturally, however, a number of difficulties arose. It was soon noticeable that the equipment and personnel were not sufficient to allow the work to be carried out as quickly as it was desirable. There was not as much transport as we would have liked. It was, of course, essential that all clearing work should be done with the greatest of care so as to avoid injuring anyone who might be still alive below the debris; but at the same time it was very desirable to get it done quickly in order to rescue those same people alive, and further to remove the dead with the utmost speed. In the Singapore climate a corpse will decay very rapidly indeed. When a normal death occurs in peace-time the body is usually buried within twelve hours. The result of this was that in cases where it took some days to dig out corpses, the neighbourhood became anything but sweet-smelling, and when the bodies were uncovered there was naturally a reluctance among men to handle them. This, I am afraid, caused differences of opinion between the personnel of the Rescue Parties and the members of the

Disposal of the Dead Squads, each organization wishing to reduce its handling of the bodies to a minimum.

Early in the proceedings it was obvious that food was also going to cause difficulties. The labour forces had usually obtained food during the course of the day's work from hawkers in the streets, but these completely disappeared on the morning after the first raid, and at that time we were not in a position to feed them by any other means; subsequently it was necessary to provide a canteen service and also to cook mass meals at the coolie lines for men returning late from work, because there was little daylight left in which they could prepare meals and of course fires and lights were forbidden after dark in the open type kitchens which alone were available. Unfortunately, we had not enough labour to work the men in shifts and keep an adequate number of men on any particular job. On the whole, however, nothing but praise can be given for the work these men did in the early days of the war. As time went on the original difficulties got ironed out, but others inevitably arose.

The other Passive Defence Services, such as the A.R.P. Wardens, the Medical Auxiliary Service, the Auxiliary Fire Service, and Volunteer Police Services were largely recruited from the clerical classes of the community, together with a number of non-British Europeans and the more influential Asiatics. So far as I could judge from personal knowledge and from hearsay, each of these Services did exceptionally good work in its own particular line, and there must be many instances of personal bravery and self sacrifice which will probably never now be known.

For a few days after the first raid my men concentrated on clearing up, but soon there was a flood of demands for other work, all to be done in a hurry. At this period the requirements of the various authorities were not centralized, and requests came in from half-a-dozen sources. It was therefore difficult to decide priority, and it was not until Brigadier Simpson was appointed Director General of Passive Defence that I was able to obtain an authoritative ruling on many questions.

As a bad example of what happened in the early stages I can cite the attempt to prevent the enemy landing planes on flat areas or sports grounds around the town. I was first asked to dig trenches six feet wide and three feet deep across all possible landing-fields, and was told that this work was of extreme urgency. Several hundred men were immediately put on the work, and trenches had been dug in a number of areas when another official stepped in and said that the trenches must not be straight, as they would undoubtedly be used for air raid shelters, and a straight trench would allow an enemy plane to machine-gun the whole lot in one sweep. It was therefore decided to fill in parts of these trenches and construct a staggered system. When this was done we were told that the excavated earth which we had originally been asked to heap on the sides of the trenches should now be removed, as a trench with a berm was an ideal prepared position for enemy parachutists. So the berms were removed and the earth dispersed. This having been duly accomplished the health authorities took a hand in the matter and said that it was suicidal from a health point of view to have trenches at all on these lands, many of which were low-lying, for mosquitoes would breed by the million. It now looked as though we would have to fill up all the trenches again, but fortunately a compromise was arrived at whereby the trenches were filled in for two feet with loose earth. This is merely given as an example of the kind of instructions which were received and of the lack of proper directions on such matters. As a matter of fact, no troop-carrying planes or parachute troops landed in Singapore, which may or may not have been due to the preparations taken.

In this crowded period we were also required to carry out security registration and compensation registration and issue identity cards, all of which might well have been done many months before. Each department did its own registration, and so added considerably to the volume of work at this trying time.

During the period between the first and second raids one saw many signs of reinforcements reaching Malta, but there was no really good news. The loss of the *Prince of Wales* and the *Repulse* put Malaya into a profound gloom and showed us the metal of which our opponents were made. The Japanese continued to advance down the Peninsula. Penang was evacuated, and many unpleasant stories were going the rounds about the fall of that island and the behaviour of the people who were resident on it. Christmas came and went, and there was little to mark its passing. Offices were open on that day, and the spirit was far from being one of peace on earth or of goodwill towards men.

CHAPTER FOUR

THINGS GETTING WORSE

ON THE EVENING OF DECEMBER 29th—that was three weeks and a few hours after the first raid—Singapore was subjected to its second bombing attack. It was a beautiful moonlight night, and when the moon is bright in Malaya visibility must be almost as good as in some daylight in many Northern countries. In times of peace we used to glory in the moonlight nights; everything looked so lovely and peaceful, but now we came to dread them, for they brought the bombers overhead. On this particular night the planes passed over near to my house and the bombs fell close enough to blow off the plywood which was nailed across the louvred windows of the lounge for black-out reasons. After the first lot of bombs had fallen there was a lull, and I thought that they had passed on, so got out my car and set out for my Rescue Station. However, I ran into trouble, and had my first baptism of bombing. I was about half a mile from the house when the search lights began to play in the sky, and by following them I could see that the planes were approaching the road on which I was driving. When they got to about the right angle for my discomfort I heard the ominous noise which I afterwards got to know so well, and which resembled the flight of doves. This, of course, was the noise of bombs falling through the air, and I hastily got out of the car and dived into a ditch half-full of muddy water. A petrol dump was hit several hundred yards away and other bombs fell nearer. I was undoubtedly comparatively safe, but for a first experience it was unpleasant.

From then on, until Singapore fell, raids were continuous, and I think there was only one period of twenty-four hours free from a raid, and most days there were several, while near the finish it was the exception rather than the rule to get a single hour without having enemy planes overhead. At first during the moonlight nights the raids were mostly at night, but soon they were supplemented by daytime raids, and we quickly got into the habit of living a shelter life. I had a shelter in the garden, built with rein forced concrete pipes sunk in a trench, which was primarily for the servants, and I also had a concrete table constructed as a shelter inside the house itself. We were urged to use the same shelter as the servants as often as possible in order to encourage and comfort them, and this we did, but at night it was easier to use the inside shelter. The sirens were not easy to hear from my residence, and so I erected a gong in the garden so that anyone who heard the siren might also beat the gong to assist in waking other people at night-time. Towards the end, the alerts at night became so frequent that it was not worthwhile going back to bed every time the all-clear sounded, so my wife and I—when off duty-slept under the concrete table in the lounge, and in this way got a much better night's sleep, as then we were not continually sleeping with one ear open, so to speak.

On the whole, the raids during the month of January were confined to military objects, and there was not a great deal of damage done to civilian property. There seemed, however, to be one or two exceptions to this rule, and on one day, in particular, there was a very heavy raid along the seafront, in the Beach Road and Connaught Drive areas. A great many bombs were dropped this day, and a great many houses were ruined. I remember visiting the area after the raid and coming away very depressed, as I realized for the first time that our Rescue and Debris Organization would not be able to tackle this raid—or other raids of similar intensity with a reasonable amount of expedition; the job was too big. As regards the Rescue Organization, one station had already been abandoned on account of bombing, another had been forced to move, first to one position and then to another, and a main Control Room for this service alone had now been established in the basement of the Municipal Offices, from which I directed the activities. The men were still doing good work, but the raids were becoming so frequent that considerable reluctance was often shown by them when they were requested to go to danger areas. No sooner would they get to an area than another raid would start, and they had to scatter for protection, taking some time to reassemble afterwards.

Various types of bombs were used by the Japanese in these raids, but on the whole they seemed to be small and a large percentage of them did not explode. Some of the high explosive bombs were filled with all types of scrap metal-bolts, springs, pieces of chain, and other miscellaneous articles were taken from wounded people. The ordinary magnesium incendiary bomb was not used, but oil bombs and sulphur bombs were; they also used anti-personnel bombs which did not explode on impact, but lay on the road looking, on end view, like a tennis ball, and only exploding by vibration from a passing car or other vehicle.

Fountain pens, dolls, and other toys filled with explosives were found on the streets, but these were, in all probability, placed there by Fifth Columnists—not dropped from aircraft.

The frequent raids, of course, greatly affected the work carried on in Singapore. People were continually running to such shelters as existed, and spending long periods in them, so that at about this time roof-spotters—otherwise known as Jim Crows—began to make their appearance on the roofs of the larger buildings with the idea of getting the staff to carry on until the spotters indicated by whistle that the planes were approaching that locality. In spite of these, however, the amount of work done in Singapore must have decreased tremendously due to the unwillingness of many to work during alert periods. Much time was spent in trying to persuade labour to work in the face of danger.

All these raids were not carried out without some opposition. There was a number of anti-aircraft batteries in and around the town, and there were some fighter aircraft to go up against the enemy. At the beginning the fighters were mainly Brewster-Buffalo machines, but these seemed to disappear very rapidly from the arena. Then came the time when we heard that Hurricane machines were soon to appear. The Hurricane—with its great record of work in the 'Battle of Britain'—seemed to us to be the answer to our troubles, and I remember very distinctly the first day they took a trial flight over Singapore and the cheers with which my neighbours greeted the sight of these hopes in the air. It may be that we did not get the latest type of Hurricane or that we did not get enough of them, or it may be that they were not suited to the climate; but whatever the cause they, too, seemed to diminish very rapidly in numbers until, at the end, they were conspicuous by their absence. They were up against a tough opponent in the Japanese Navy 'O' fighter.

There was nothing in the course of the war in these days to give us any hope. Taiping fell; then Ipoh. We thought the enemy would be held in the Slim River area, but he seemed to be scarcely even checked. Next, Kuala Lumpur fell, and we heard grand stories about the completeness of the scorched earth policy, especially in that town; but there was nothing very consoling about that. The towns between Kuala Lumpur and the Maur River were taken by the enemy in rapid succession, and we now hoped that a stand would be made at this river. The biggest battle of the campaign was, I think, fought here, and the enemy was temporarily brought to a standstill, but soon the Japanese infiltrated behind our lines, and again we were in retreat.

Infiltration, the new word in the jargon of war, became a bogy to us; always the enemy was infiltrating behind our lines, and always we were retreating to re-establish these lines. We recognized that it was entirely possible for twenty, two hundred, or two thousand Japanese to get behind our lines comparatively easily and possibly disorganize them from the rear, but we did not recognize why it was not possible for twenty, two hundred or two thousand of the British Forces to get behind the Japanese lines and stop their advance. However, that appeared to be the case, and advance they did and very rapidly. There were, of course, difficulties on our side which must not be minimized. Many of the British troops were very new to the country, and did not recognize the difference between Japanese, Chinese, Malays, and even Indians. This was by no means always an easy thing to do, even for an old resident, and it was certainly impossible in the case of troops newly in the country. The Japanese played on this, and disguised

31

themselves as Chinese, Malays, and Indians who might be considered as residents of the villages and towns, and, helped by these disguises, penetrated through our lines with results which can be imagined. Our troops were also unwisely, I think, required to carry heavy equipment and were clothed in a comparatively heavy manner for a tropical country, whereas the Japs were clothed in the very lightest of garments, such as a vest, a pair of pants, and canvas shoes, and carried very little equipment per man, which gave them much greater mobility in a country covered with jungle and swamp.

After the battle at the Maur River I do not think anyone expected the enemy to be held on the mainland. He made further landings on the east coast, and also advanced quickly southward, so it was apparent that, at the best, Singapore would be subjected to a siege.

Thinking back on this period there are many things which come to mind. One noticed the complete cessation of almost all forms of normal life. At first the rush to get things done and then gradually the feeling that nothing was worth doing. More and more people were being bombed out of homes and offices and were seeking alternative accommodation. More and more cars and lorries were being requisitioned for military needs. More and more of one's friends and acquaintances were being killed or wounded. People looked ill, and the town was getting dirty and dilapidated. The damage could no longer be cleared quickly; and the roads, in which I prided myself, were showing many signs of neglect. It was all a desolate sight and pulled at the heart-strings of those who had watched Singapore grow. Much advice was being given by the newspapers and on the radio about air-raid precautions, and information about Japanese methods was being

Part of the Singapore Waterfront

Singapore Railway Station

The Esplanade, Singapore

broadcast, and there were also appeals for assistance of all kinds. Much of this was out of date almost before it was uttered, so rapidly did things happen, so quickly did the scene change.

Until the Japanese landed on the island I believed Singapore could be held. It will never be possible to say how many shared my view, but certainly many of my friends did not. I know, intimately, men who held from the beginning that Singapore would fall. To their credit be it said that this did not in any way impair their war efforts. In fact, I knew men who were spending their normal furlough in Australia or South Africa and who—although believing that Malaya could not hold—yet rushed back to lend what assistance they could before the finish. From some points of view this was a noble gesture, but from others it was surely a very foolish one, because it meant that more man-power and more talent was to be locked up in Singapore until peace was declared. This being the case, it seems hard to understand why reinforcements were poured into Singapore almost to the end, for many troops ended their career of usefulness to the Empire in this war by being captured in the fallen city.

We, who believed that Singapore could be held, were much shaken by Churchill's speech, which told us to expect further reverses, and said ominously little about Singapore itself. This speech discouraged many people. A lady whom I knew very well had been badly injured by blast from a bomb, and when I visited her in hospital on the morning that the speech was reported in the newspapers she was telling her husband that the next time she wished to be killed outright, because "Churchill has given Singapore up".

On the other hand, the Governor of the Colony, Sir Shenton Thomas, said "Singapore must not, will not, fall."

The Governor at this time was being criticized on many grounds, I think unjustly. He and General Percival were left to carry the burden of the day, and on the principle that a cat may look at a king, I may say on slight acquaintance with these two men that they were both loyalty and democracy in its best forms, and they always treated even the humblest with the greatest respect. By the time January had gone many who held high ranks in political, Naval, Military, and Air circles and whose names had been splashed across Malaya's visitors' book had gone also. The Governor and General Percival were left to nurse Malaya in its death struggles.

Early in the war Penang fell. It seemed that the town was heavily bombed, and as there were few shelters many of the populace, largely the labouring classes, rushed out of the town to the countryside and stayed there. The result was disorganization of the distribution of food and essential supplies, and much misery was caused. The defences of Penang were poor, and the Military Authorities, not the Civil Government, asked the Europeans and others to evacuate. Later, this caused a storm of protest, as it was alleged that, when the Japanese came, there were few in authority to establish civil order and arrange the proper functioning of services essential to the welfare of the Asiatic community who remained. As an outcome of this it was stated that in future civil servants would remain in occupied towns and districts, and the Governor said over the radio that while the Government would evacuate as many women and children as possible, there was no question of the Europeans running away and leaving the Asiatic. The wisdom of adhering rigidly to this policy may be questioned, but I believe he tried to stick to it. Many European men did leave in the end, but I suspect he was persuaded to agree to this, if, indeed, he was entirely aware of it, by great pressure and by the reasonableness of many arguments. He had, I take it, no say in the evacuation of the many members of the Services who left the island at an earlier or later date. This would be in the hands of the Service chiefs.

So far as I am aware no compulsion was used to evacuate women and children from the Colony, and up to near the end they were required to pay their own passages if they wished to get out. Many did so and left comparatively early; others stayed and said they would never go; and still others put their names down for passages, hoping that before these were available the news would be better.

Towards the end of January, as things continued to get worse, I persuaded my wife to put her name down for a passage, and our neighbour, Mrs. Kelly, did likewise. Two days later, January 30th, the enemy were nearing the Johore Straits. That morning my wife, who had been doing voluntary work daily with the Blood Transfusion Service— which had been rendering excellent service under the efficient guidance of Dr. G. V. Allen—was trying to get in touch with some of her co-workers by telephone. She found that they had almost all gone or were packing to leave. Stories of the atrocities committed in Hong Kong went through my mind, and I decided that it was time that she should go also. On telephoning to the shipping company's office, they informed us that a passage could be obtained on a large ship, and passengers must be aboard within a few hours. My wife and Mrs. Kelly secured passages and were allowed to take a cabin trunk and a suitcase each. That morning the docks were severely damaged and the normal route to the ship was barred by fires; so an alternative route, using a small boat across the Empire Dock, had to be taken

37

and we had to handle our own luggage. The docks were crammed with cars of thousands of people evacuating; this must have been a large percentage of the women and children left in Singapore. It was a desperately anxious afternoon. We were watching the skies all the time for further raids. A raid on the docks that after noon would have been attended by a holocaust. Women and children embarking on the ships would have been slaughtered by thousands. As it happened there was an alert, but the planes did not come over that particular part of the town. Mr. Kelly (known to his friends as Sid) and I spent an anxious night wondering if the ship got away safely. The next morning I went down to the docks and found it had remained there all night, and was just setting off. I learnt later that it was attacked by an aeroplane off Java, but escaped damage or casualties, eventually reaching Great Britain safely. The passengers were anything but comfortable, and were sleeping in hundreds on mattresses on the deck and doing their own washing-up and cleaning in addition to many ship's chores.

This ship sailed on Saturday, January 31st, and for a week after that there was a comparative lull, because that morning the Causeway, which joined Singapore Island to the mainland and which carried the road and railway, had been breached and Singapore was once more, after twenty years, an island in fact as well as in name. The Japanese were on the other side of the Straits of Johore, separated from the island by three-quarters of a mile of water. The lull remained while they were preparing for their attack on the island itself.

CHAPTER FIVE

THE LAST FORTNIGHT

THUS IN LESS THAN EIGHT WEEKS Japan had conquered the whole of the Peninsula, and had established herself in Johore Bahm, the capital of the Johore state, at the extreme southern tip facing Singapore Island. Just across the intervening Straits was the world famed Naval Base, the cost of which was probably not less than one hundred million pounds. Part of the equipment of the Base was a floating dock and a dry-dock, both, I believe, the second largest of their kind in the world. The Base was now useless, and probably had been since the outbreak of war.

Within ten miles of Japanese occupied territory were countless military objectives on the island, such as camps, aerodromes, oil tanks, ammunition dumps, and all the paraphernalia of war, and about fifteen miles away, as the crow flies, was the town of Singapore.

During the first week of February we were naturally trying feverishly to strengthen the Fortress, including the defences on the north side of the island, Singapore's back door, and the Japanese were bringing down reinforcements, guns, and supplies to the territory on the other side of the dividing channel. Activity was confined to artillery fire and air raids. Some of Singapore's aerodromes, being under fire, were unusable or nearly so, and our fighter machines must have been compelled to use one aerodrome almost exclusively: that was the former civil airport at Kallang, on the south coast near the town, and even this was being attacked from the air with alarming frequency. How many planes we had at this time I do not know, but there seemed to be very few indeed, and the enemy appeared to do pretty much as he liked in the air.

The island now presented an amazing sight. There were troops and camps and guns almost every few yards; all the forces which had formerly been scattered over the considerable area of the mainland were now concentrated on the island in an area of about two hundred and six square miles, much of it swamp. In addition to the troops, many of the civilians of all races had retreated to Singapore in front of the foe so that troops in all conditions of fatigue and dirt were seeking camps, and civilians were seeking accommodation. All usable transport, tanks, guns, agricultural and engineering plant—and even domestic animals—had joined the march, and they were all in Singapore. Day and night traffic on wheels, rollers, and caterpillars streamed over the roads looking for a resting-place. Guns were put in every conceivable position, and cattle were turned on to the former golf courses and playing fields. Whatever was the cause of Singapore's fall it cannot have been the lack of troops or transport.

When our wives left Singapore on January 31st I moved into Sid Kelly's house to live with him, as his house was farther from the main road than mine and so quieter under the conditions prevailing. I took a lot of my household stuff with me, including the stocks of food and drink which we had been advised to store against the possibilities of a siege or breakdown in distribution. The rest of my goods I put in cases and sent to a store in town.

I had known Sid for twelve years and we were good friends. He was a good engineer, an excellent golfer, and a generous friend. He was fond of the good things of life, especially good food, but he was a confirmed pessimist, at least so far as the war in Malaya was concerned. He was not, perhaps, the most cheerful person to talk to at nights, although he did laugh at his own pessimism, but I set it off against my tendency to wishful thinking, and probably arrived at a reasonable view. He was attached to the Municipal Water Department, and during this time was kept busy repairing damage to pumping and supply lines and preparing them for worse to come. Indeed, at this time, all of us in the Municipal essential services were meeting with great difficulties, as the damage being caused was greater than we could deal with expeditiously. The labour force was very reluctant to work in dangerous conditions, and the conditions were practically always likely to be dangerous. In spite of the multitude of motor vehicles which had come to the island, forty Municipal lorries were commandeered for military requirements, and many of these had to come from my rescue work, which did not make that job any easier.

About this time some chlorine arrived on a ship for use in the Municipal water supply, and there were difficulties about unloading it. Sid found it necessary to pay several visits to the docks, and on return he told me something of the conditions prevailing there. Apparently there was very little or no ordinary labour available for unloading ships, and this work was being done largely by British and Indian soldiers, mostly at night. He also found that members of the R.A.F. were being evacuated in order to staff aerodromes in the Dutch East Indies. Others were going for various reasons, some were forming crews for ships where the native crews had deserted, and others were leaving ostensibly to take up important work in other theatres.

I think it was this which first brought to our minds the idea that if Singapore was going to fall we might perhaps escape internment, and we subsequently found that we were well behind in that line of thought. Many had already been struck by the uselessness of handing themselves over. They had done their alloted tasks as long as it was possible, but now it was no longer possible. They could not get to the firing line and there was nothing more they could do here. There was a job for them in other theatres.

In the backs of people's minds there had always been the possibility of a siege and, judging by instructions issued from time to time by the Government, that was also the official view, but the Japanese thought otherwise; they apparently never contemplated trying to starve Singapore out, and even from the beginning were out to take it by storm.

The first move in the attack came as a surprise. On Saturday morning, February 7th, the town was shelled from the mainland of Johore, the shells falling in the Orchard Road and Bukit Timah Road areas, about two miles from the centre of the town. This was long-range shooting, and the shells were not very big, but in many ways they were more terrifying than the bombs, for one had no indication of when they would come over. There was more shelling again on Sunday morning, and it was very widespread.

On Sunday night I was on duty at the Rescue Parties' Control Room in the Municipal Offices; I spent one night in three on such duty. This was the night of the great bombardment; the Japanese had now established their artillery in and around Johore Bahru, and this night they furiously bombarded the shores on the north and west of the island. I climbed with a friend to the top of the Municipal Offices and from the flat roof watched this terrific duel for some time. I have nothing with which to compare it, but I know that next day men who had fought in France in 1914-18 had long arguments as to whether or not this bombardment exceeded in intensity anything which they had seen in that war. To me it sounded terrific, and apparently it succeeded in its object of driving our forces back from the coast, at least at one point, and later that night the Japanese landed at this point. The battle for Singapore had begun.

All Monday we hoped against hope for news that the enemy had been driven back into the sea off the island. It did not come. In fact, further landings were effected on Monday night, and as soon as they had gained a firm foothold guns were brought across, and, from then on, Singapore was under continual shell fire. There had been, of course, fires from time to time in the town and all over the island caused by enemy action, but now that the Japanese were on Singapore, oil tanks and other supplies on the north of the island were set alight by our own forces to deny them to the enemy. Great volumes of smoke filled the skies and spread like a cloud over the town and surrounding country. The tropical sun was obscured behind a dense black mantle. It was the most depressing sky I have ever seen or ever want to see, and it remained thus for days.

Things were getting hot around our house, and as some of our own guns were stationed nearby retaliatory shells were coming uncomfortably close. We had also been just missed by several bombs, but we still ate and slept there. At tiffin on Monday we had with us a junior officer of the Malayan

R.N.V.R. He had been accustomed to make the house his headquarters when off duty. He told us more details of what was happening in the harbour. He himself was ordered away that evening and he told us how we might escape if we felt so inclined. We recognized the folly and uselessness of staying, and were sorely tempted, but everything we had in the world was tied up in Singapore, and to go, while there might still be left something which we could do, was not to our liking though we saw clearly our usefulness was drawing to an end. We would also, of course, lose everything; but by that time we expected to lose that anyhow.

Tuesday morning brought certain instructions which, for me, put the seal on everything and quenched the last spark of hope that Singapore would hold. I was instructed to have very important machinery belonging to the department destroyed to deny it to the enemy. I reasoned that the authorities knew the end was coming, for otherwise this machinery, which was of great importance to the community and to the war effort, should have been preserved. I am afraid these instructions depressed me more than anything that had hitherto happened. Sixteen years of my life had been spent in playing, to the best of my ability, my humble part in building up the Singapore which was being blown to pieces, and the greedy maw of war now required even the destruction of tools with which I had built. Sid and I discussed it at midday. Was there anything we could do about it? There did not seem to be, nor did it seem possible for us to help in any way more than we were doing. Sid frankly thought that the policy of holding out 'to the last drop of blood', as the phrase went, was criminal in the destruction of property and loss of life it caused. Singapore was finished, he said, and it would be much better to admit it and save all the life and property possible. I did not agree, as at that time I still subscribed to the thought that every hour's delay was of value in the larger field. We were, however, in complete agreement that, as Singapore was to fall, all the man-power and material possible should be got away from it so that they might be available to fight again. We thought particularly of all the skilled men whom the Municipality employed, and how they would be rendered useless to the Empire for the rest of the war. We would, however, do nothing about it, but we determined to try that afternoon to find out as best we could how the land lay; there was no point in just waiting for others to think and plan for us; we knew the futility of that. Perhaps we were impatient and self-opinionated, but that self-same impatience was a good ally in days to come.

That afternoon we went a tour of the docks or as near as we could get to them. They were, of course, protected areas, and permits were necessary, but, in places, the guard was no longer kept. I think that by this time many of the Harbour Board Staff had left and the docks were largely in charge of the Army. We saw ships lying alongside and men in uniform coming and going. Obviously, more Military and Air Force personnel were leaving.

At Clifford Pier—which we visited last—we met, by chance, some of the European staff of a well-known firm. We knew them as friends and we talked to them. They told us that the battle on the west coast of the island was a debacle and our forces were in retreat. General Wavell had been in Singapore for a few hours and had left—or was leaving—soon by air. They saw only misfortune in that. They themselves had been asked to man a small ship, they told us, bound for Australia, and they thought we should get out. If we were prepared to help as crew we could come with them, either now or any time up till three a.m. next morning.

"Well," I said to Sid, "it is a good offer, and it's up to us to find out what the powers that be think of it. I for one wouldn't consider going without the President's permission, although it's obviously foolish to stay here and be caught like rats in a trap."

The Municipal President in Singapore is a senior civil servant seconded as Chairman of the Board of Commissioners, and at the same time he is Senior Executive Officer. All dealings between the staff and the Commissioners or the Government are carried on through him.

We drove immediately to his residence in Ridout Road and asked to see him. Fortunately he was alone, and received us at once. I told him I wished to speak to him as man to man about the situation. It was obvious to us that Singapore was falling, was there any policy about the Municipal staff? Would it be evacuated or could anyone who was able to do so save himself? We had had, I said, the offer of a passage, but we would not take it without his permission. We held very strongly that we would be much more use out of Singapore than as prisoners within, possibly helping the enemy to run Singapore in his own interests. He received all this very sympathetically, but said that it was not certain that Singapore was going to fall; at least, he could tell us that instructions had been issued that morning at nine a.m. to destroy certain assets, but these instructions had been cancelled at eleven a.m. I think he referred to the currency and, if so, he was mistaken as to the reason for this alteration. In any case, he said, he had no authority to give us permission to go. He, in his position, had to stay, and others whom he mentioned by name were

46

staying. If we did go, however, we should take certain documents with us. He thought the Imperial Government had let Malaya down, but he also thought it was disgraceful how Malayan civil servants had left up-country towns before they were occupied. This was our ship, he said, and we should stick to it.

I quite agreed that this was our ship, and so long as there was the slightest hope of saving it my life and everything I had was at its service, but no ship I had ever heard of had required its crew to deliberately drown themselves once the ship was gone beyond hope. If he could do so, everyone was entitled to save himself by swimming. All we wanted was his blessing on an attempt to save ourselves when our ship had foundered.

We talked further on the possible fate of our life savings and of what was likely to happen when the Japanese arrived. He thought the accounts of Japanese atrocities were exaggerated, and imagined that we would be asked to run our jobs for a few weeks until they got their own men, and then we would possibly be shipped to Formosa. He added, jokingly, that he would like to see Formosa. Sid replied that he would not see much of it from behind barbed wire.

Before leaving we both told him that in view of what he had said we would put the matter of leaving completely out of our minds. From the look he gave us I still think he was sorry even then that the result of the interview had not been otherwise.

I hope I have recorded this interview correctly in substance, for I owe a great deal to Mr. Rayman, the President, and I would be loath to misrepresent him in any way.

We went back to our house and shortly afterwards the guns on both sides began to send across their steel messages of death, and there were enemy planes overhead. We endured it for a while, but it looked as if it was going to be an all-night show, and we decided that, as it was impossible to sleep there, we would pack a case and go down to the Municipal Offices and try to get some rest. We hurriedly finished dinner amid an infernal racket, and then took a perilous drive down to the office, perilous on account of the shell fire and of the extreme darkness of the night.

We arrived there to find that others were coming in also, for many of the suburbs were becoming untenantable. The Municipal Offices, a modern reinforced concrete five-story building, was situated on the southern sea-front in the heart of the town, so was about as far from the enemy as anywhere at that time.

In the basement of the offices various departments which dealt with essential services had control rooms to where all incidents were reported, and from where all repair work was organized. There were camp-beds and mattresses and, until the end, most officers dealing with these services lived in the building, eating and sleeping in the control-room or in their own private offices.

That night there was much discussion of the probabilities and possibilities of the situation, and many showed that they would like very much to get away if it were possible, and if they had the courage to take the risk, for they were no longer any use in Singapore; but many others were fearful of what might happen to all their possessions if they did manage to make a getaway. We said nothing; we did not wish to influence anyone in any direction. It was a decision everyone must make for himself. We had made our bed and we were going to lie on it.

We thought that the end had come that night because there was firing very close at hand on the beach to the east

Raffles Place, Singapore

Municipal Buildings, Singapore

of us. This, we learned subsequently, was an attempted landing near Bedok, which, however, was repulsed. We spent a considerable time in planning what was the best way to meet the situation should the Japanese walk into the building.

Wednesday was a dreadful day. More and more people with tales of disaster were coming into the building for refuge. Soldiers of the British and Australian Forces who had lost their units came in and hung around the basement corridors, as also did Asiatics from the neighbouring streets. The noise of shell fire was incessant and air raids were continuous.

There were no newspapers, and rumour was very busy and took the wildest forms. The following are some examples:

- 125,000 Americans had landed in Penang;
- The Chinese were advancing down through Thailand;
- A large number of Japanese ships had been sunk in the Bay of Bengal;
- Wavell had said "hold on for two days and everything will be all right";
- The Japs had been pushed back to the Causeway.

Of the above remarks (1) and (2) were entirely unfounded. Some ships may have been sunk at that time, I do not know, but if so it might account for rumour (3). As regards (4), some military officers afterwards told me that General Wavell had made the statement attributed to him, but it may not be so.

As regards the rumour that the Japanese had been pushed back to the Causeway, we subsequently learnt that an attack

51

had been made by our forces, which drove the enemy back a considerable distance, but not quite so far as rumour had it.

While we were living in the building, Sid and I each morning went on a trip to our house to collect clothes and food. We chose the early morning, as it was always quietest, but even so we generally had to stop the car once or twice and lie in a ditch for a bit or shoot dangerous stretches of road at top speed.

One of our Chinese servants was still living in the shelter at the house which, so far, had not been touched. The loyalty and courage with which many Chinese and Malay servants stood to their employers in these days is worthy of all praise. So far as my knowledge goes, the Asiatic population of Singapore was, to the end, loyal and helpful on the whole.

On the way back to the office on Wednesday morning we dropped into one of the workshops and saw the pathetic sight of men gazing wistfully at the machinery which we had broken up the night before. These were the machines on which they had worked, the machines which had been their livelihood. That morning I also saw the last British aeroplane I was to see in the skies of Singapore; it was circling over Kallang Airport, doubtless preparatory to leaving for the Netherland East Indies.

That afternoon the Municipal subordinate staff was paid two months' salary in advance. Different departments paid their own employees on this occasion, and I was handed $47,000 for the Municipal Engineer's Department. During the next two days I spent a good deal of time paying this out, as many of our staff worked outside and could only get in if things quietened down for a bit. Many never got in. This advance payment was only another sign that the end was coming and the authorities wished the banks cleared of money. It was a good move, as it ensured the residents' money in the days immediately following the fall of Singapore—if money was any good to them.

The Japanese had been using, since they landed in Malaya, notes similar to Straits currency, superscribed with the words 'The Government of Japan promises to pay the Bearer', which is just another example of their preparedness.

Wednesday evening appeared to me to be more cheerful than the day which had preceded it, largely, I think, on account of the news now fairly well confirmed that our Forces had successfully counter-attacked and forced the Japanese back on the island, and also on account of Wavell's alleged promise that there would be help in two days. In some of us hope even revived that the brand might be snatched from the fire at the last moment.

Thursday, however, brought disillusionment; things were as bad as ever or worse. The Japanese were again advancing and were getting very close to the town.

The Military Authorities were asked to clear the building of soldiers who were sheltering there, but this was never completely done. The town was full of troops; lost, hungry, dirty, and exhausted, and looking for somewhere to rest in comparative peace. Hospitals on the outskirts were becoming untenantable and new sites were being commandeered in the centre of the town and the wounded moved in. Among other buildings the Singapore Cricket Club and the Cathedral became hospitals.

My Rescue Parties could no longer operate from their stations, and all that could be done was to keep a few gangs at the Municipal Offices and send them out from there. During these days my two chief assistant-engineers, Mr.

Weston and Mr. O'Toole, did amazing work and took endless risks in the cause of this Passive Defence work.

There were no longer any air raid warnings, there was a continuous red message on my table which meant a continual period of alert. Sometimes the bombs fell near, sometimes farther away, but always seemed to be coming down. There was a good deal of anti-aircraft fire which increased the noise, but it did not prevent continual raids. There was also never-ending shell fire from both sides to add to the inferno.

Among other places Government House was hit by a shell that evening just after dark, and I received a message asking for a Rescue Party. It proved impossible to get any ordinary gangs, so I chased around among Municipal officers and officers of the Public Works Department who had that day come into the Municipal Offices for safety, their own offices having been bombed previously. I eventually got a dozen or so Municipal officers who went out in private cars as a rescue squad to Government House, but fortunately there was little to do.

That night there was no cheerfulness, there was nothing but an air of complete despair and hopelessness. There were no newspapers and little news over the radio, but we did not need these services to know how things were going. People who came in from the outskirts of the town told us that the battle was approaching such and such a spot. These spots were, as time went on, getting nearer and nearer to the heart of the city. Apart from anything else the noise confirmed this. Those of us who sought rest that night did so with a heavy heart; it seemed to be the end of everything.

CHAPTER SIX

FRIDAY THE 13TH

TO THE SUPERSTITIOUS FRIDAY THE 13TH is an unlucky day. I do not believe that I thought of it at all at the time, but I have many times since, and I am still undecided whether or not it was unlucky for me, though unquestionably it was momentous.

This day commenced for me when I was awakened from a fitful sleep to take a spell of duty at the front door of the Municipal Offices. It had been found necessary to man this door to keep crowds of unauthorized people from entering and taking up their abode inside. It was crowded enough as it was. I spent a long and weary two hours sitting in the gloomy foyer trying to keep awake and guessing where that one fell as the bombs came down. I do not remember exactly what I thought about, but my thoughts cannot have been very comforting. Nothing could be more dismal than waiting for the end in a situation like this. So far as I could see a long internment awaited me among people of a coloured race who inevitably had different standards and different methods of thought from mine. In the meantime my wife and child would have no means of support. When the war ended and if I had come through alive it would not be easy, at my age, to start again in a post-war world. This was bound to be the fate of many, and the early hours of the morning did not make it appear any more attractive.

In those grim hours, death seemed almost the best solution, yet even that would only be a solution as far as I myself was concerned. With telegraphic communication broken down or fully engaged, news of my death would not get out and my family would be kept in uncertainty as many other families afterwards were. Indeed death was an ever-present possibility and it seemed to be much a matter of luck. One of my assistant-engineers had on two occasions been within twenty-five feet of the spot where a bomb fell and had been saved by seemingly inadequate protection. My own office had had several splinters come through the window, and often when going round my work trying to encourage my officers and men I had been caught in the open with no protection while bombs were falling not far away. Yes, it seemed a matter of luck, a few yards this way or that and one's problems would be solved.

When daylight came Sid and I, as usual, prepared to make our trip to the house. When we were getting his car from the garage two soldiers in a wretched state appeared and asked us for water. We told them to get into the car and we would get them food and drink. At the house we had tea and food prepared, which was eaten between dashes for shelter. They had had little food for days and were delighted with the hot tea and good food. They were very careful not to sit on the cushioned chairs, fearing their dirty condition would soil the fabrics. This amused us vastly, for what did cushioned chairs matter, they would soon belong to someone else. In fact we never saw them again.

While the soldiers ate we poured all the spirits and other drink we had down the drain, which we had been asked to do, as it was reported that drink found by the Japanese in

Hong Kong had been responsible for many atrocities. A vast amount of alcohol in one form or another must have gone down the drains that week and all the sewer rats must have had a merry time. Following the example set by many employers we gave the one servant who remained a large advance of pay and then loaded up our car with food and clothes in case we had to stay indefinitely at the office. The car loaded, we started the return journey, and even Sid's dog seemed to know it would be our last appearance, for he ran after us as far as his ancient legs would carry him. It was a broken journey back, but we arrived there, gave some food to the soldiers, bade them good-bye and good luck.

The morning passed as others had done in doing any job which came to hand, and in discussing the situation with all and sundry to find if anyone had any news. We looked in vain for any glimmer of hope.

My rescue work had by now collapsed. The men, or rather those who had not already disappeared, could not be persuaded to face the dangers of the streets. I had previously made several abortive attempts to get supplementary labour, and now the only men available were a few more highly paid and better educated men who had formerly worked in Kuala Lumpur on the same job. They could do very little, and the great majority of the incidents must have been left unattended except for what neighbours could do. I think that all the Passive Defence Services had, by this time, crumbled. The cemeteries were now virtually in the front line and disposal of the dead became a tragic problem. I spent hours on the telephone and rushing about trying to see if anything could be done, but it was impossible. Fortunately the telephone was still working, in the town area at least, and the water and electricity supplies were still available except where broken mains or cables had interrupted them locally. Our building was hit by a shell, but little damage was done.

It was about 2.30 p.m. that a messenger came to me from the President to say that he wanted to see Kelly and myself in his office. I immediately guessed that it was in connection with our previous visit to him, and I wondered if he had now changed his mind about the advisability of remaining to be captured. If so, I did not know what I would do as an attempt to escape might now be suicidal.

The President and Mr. James Stone, the Municipal Treasurer, awaited us, and the former came to the point immediately by reminding us that we had come to him a few days ago with the object of finding out whether there was any question of evacuating Municipal officers. We had told him, he said, that we considered we would be more use outside than we could possibly be interned in Singapore, but what he had then said had prevented us from going.

"Well," he continued, "the position is now bad, in fact it is desperate. There are two small ships leaving to-night in an endeavour to get to Batavia. They expect to travel by night and hide among the islands by day. I have here two passes signed by Brigadier Simpson which you can have if you care to take the risk of going. If you go you must be on board before 5 p.m., and you can only take one suitcase in which you should carry enough food for six days."

There was silence while we assimilated this and then he spoke again.

"If you do not want to go you will lose nothing by staying, and if you do go you will lose nothing by going; you go with my permission. I do not know what the chances are of getting through, it will not be a pleasant journey. You must decide quickly."

"Are there others going?" I asked him.

The Road and Railway down the Malay Peninsula

The Causeway Joining Singapore to the Mainland

The Floating Dock at Singapore Naval Base

"Yes, there will be plenty of others," he said.

"Will we be letting anyone down by going; is there anything more we can do here?" I asked further.

"No," he replied emphatically.

Hesitating a few seconds, I said: "All right, sir, I will take the chance."

Sid did not make up his mind at once. I think he would have liked to weigh up the pros and cons carefully and to find out all possible details about the ship and what it proposed doing, but the President would not, or could not, give him any more information.

He said: "I doubt if I want to."

The President then asked if there was anyone else he could suggest who might wish to take the chance. Sid suggested a name, but it did not seem very acceptable to Mr. Rayman.

During the hesitation which followed I turned to Sid and said as persuasively as I could: "Sid, let us take it; it will be an adventure." A moment's delay followed, then he said: "All right."

The President then produced the two passes and asked for our full names, which he filled in on them. He told us how to get to the ship and said we must tell no one, not even the heads of our respective departments, nor was anyone to see us going.

We shook hands with him and Mr. Stone. To Mr. Rayman I said: "Thank you, sir, and good luck." "Good luck, Gilmour," he replied.

During the interview we had to take refuge twice in the passage, and several times jumped or ducked as explosions occurred nearby.

To this moment I do not know how Mr. Rayman got these passes or why, but I will be ever grateful to him for the opportunity he gave us that day, even though there was a long way to go before freedom was to be ours.

Sid and I then held a council of war. It was not going to be easy to pack our suitcases and get away without being seen. We decided to go at once, as the longer we stayed the more chance there was of our intentions being discovered and, in view of what the President said, we did not wish that to happen.

I had to return to the Control Room and there met Mr. Fyfe, the Municipal Engineer, who had heard that the President had sent for me. He enquired why and I had to lie to him. Neither in peace or war did we always see eye to eye, but I was very sorry to think that my last statement to him was a lie. There was nothing for it, however; the President had been most emphatic that he should not be told. Later, I met a Chinese clerk who was a particularly good clerk and a particularly good fellow. He had done his job and any other I asked of him all through. Now he wanted to make certain arrangements for the next morning. It wasn't easy to tell him I would do this and that, knowing I would not, and I had an almost uncontrollable desire to shake hands and wish him luck-but that would have been contrary to my instructions.

We got out of a basement exit and drove in Sid's car to the wharves. Sid gave his car, an almost new Chevrolet, as a present to the surprised soldier at the gate. It was an empty gift, as twenty minutes later it was blown to pieces

We found there was a large crowd of people at the wharf waiting, like ourselves, to get on to one of the several ships which were to try to get through. The crowd was a mixture of civilians and Services, and it contained a large number of women and some children. Most of the women, but not all, were from the staffs of the hospitals and were being evacuated at this last moment.

These people were being taken to the ships on small launches, and on the launch to which we were allocated there were a number of sisters and nurses, European, Eurasian, and Chinese; many of these young girls were terribly frightened, and some of them, religiously inclined, were weeping and praying by turns, others were trying to comfort them by saying that all their troubles were now over, a promise which subsequently proved far from being correct. We got to the ship, and while awaiting other boatloads of people we were twice bombed. On one occasion a number of people were killed on the wharf which we had just left, and on the other occasion the bombs, while missing the ship, were near enough to kill four people on board and wound a number of others. Every one was helping where he could, the men formed a chain to get the suitcases on board and to assist the women. At first many had been cheerful and relieved at the prospect of getting away from the incessant bombing and shelling, but the bombs which came so near us and caused casualties on board damped most of their cheerfulness. The more thoughtful knew that they were taking a desperate risk. By remaining in Singapore they would most likely retain life if not freedom, by leaving they gambled heavily with life itself.

Just as it was getting dark we steamed out of the harbour, and I remember being irritated by the fact that the ship was facing the wrong way and took so long to turn when it might easily have been turned before the passengers got on board. There was enough light left for those who felt so inclined to take a last look at the town which had meant so much to them. Here they had made their lives; here their lives had been broken up. None of us, I think, doubted in ultimate victory;

but Singapore could never be the same again to those who had been through the last fortnight, to those who saw it now.

Little of the actual destruction could be seen from our position at sea. The main docks, which had been terribly battered, were round the corner; the native quarters were back from the water front; and the most badly damaged areas were also farther inland. The bombers had, in the main, spared the big buildings along the front; perhaps they wanted these for themselves.

A number of fires could be seen raging throughout the town and thick smoke clouded large sections of the sky. The oil islands of Pulo Bukum, Pulo Sambo, and Pulo Saborah in front of us were sheets of flame, rising as if in wrath from the dark blue waters. I was afterwards told that thirty-six million pounds' worth of oil was destroyed on the first two alone. The sunset was living up to its traditions of beauty and the whole presented a fantastic sight.

Light slipped into darkness, searchlights from the shore played across the sea keeping a watchful eye on the southern front, the blazing islands ahead lighted our path as we left Singapore, the last time for many, perhaps for all.

As the darkness increased and the fires were left behind, our fears of aerial attack diminished and we looked around for means to make ourselves as comfortable as possible for the night. We selected a corner of the deck, or rather we took the only place we could find, so crowded was the ship, and there settled down on our coats. It was far from comfortable, but we congratulated ourselves on our good fortune and felt freer in mind and body than we had done for a long time. Our optimism was certainly unjustified, but tired as we were it helped us to fall into an early sleep.

CHAPTER SEVEN

SUNK

IN THESE REGIONS THE NORTH-EAST MONSOON prevails from October till about March. It is a comparatively cold wind which often blows with great strength. On this night it was not very strong but it was chilly, and the cold woke us up or at least assisted the hard deck to do so. We went below into the hold, and I found a vacant spot on some sacks of merchandize where I was able to get snatches of sleep till daylight.

The ship had stopped not far from an island and was awaiting light to go in closer, which she soon did, and anchored about four hundred yards from the island which we afterwards got to know was called Pompong. This island was composed entirely of a hill with very steep sides; the top of the hill may have been three hundred feet above sea-level. The whole island was covered with dense jungle and was uninhabited; the shore was fringed with sharp, jagged rocks of volcanic origin except for a short sandy stretch on the east side. It was not at all a pleasant-looking island.

Sid and I breakfasted off a tin of salmon and half a loaf of bread which we had brought with us. As we sat on the top deck eating this we noticed another ship anchored some two hundred and fifty yards away and nearer the shore. This was the *Tien Kwang*, which was evacuating people from Singapore in the same way as our ship was. We were on the

Kuala. Still another ship was lying about two miles away; she looked not quite right, being a bit down at the stern and we wondered what she was. She was, as we afterwards learnt, the *Kung Wo,* which had left Singapore in company with the *Shu Kwang* the day before. Both were bombed, but the former had not sunk although hit. The *Shu Kwang* had gone to the bottom. The survivors of both ships were at that moment on an island behind us, waiting to be rescued. Before long a launch came alongside our ship to tell us what had happened to the *Kung Wo* and *Shu Kwang* and to ask us to take their survivors on board. This, I believe, our captain agreed to do after dark that evening.

On board our ship was the majority of the Malayan Public Works Department. These engineers, when their ordinary work became impossible, had recently been gazetted as officers in the Straits Settlements Volunteer Force. They were all in khaki, with ranks varying according to the positions they had held in civil life. The Director of Public Works, Mr. R. L. Nunn, was in charge of them; he wore the stripes of a group-captain, which rank he had held for some time in the Malayan Volunteer Air Force.

Group-Captain Nunn now organized his P.W.D. officers and such others as were willing to do a job, into working parties. These parties were to clean the ship and put things in order as far as possible, but the special job allotted them was to attempt to camouflage the ship by foliage cut from the jungle on shore and draped around the ship. Boats have undoubtedly been camouflaged in this manner and made to look like small islands such as are quite a common feature in these waters. It is, however, a big job, and the bigger the ship the bigger the job. Our ship was, I suppose, at least eleven hundred tons and it takes a lot of branches to cover eleven hundred tons of ship effectively.

The job, nevertheless, got started. A few lifeboats were lowered and working parties sent ashore to cut branches and load them on to the boats. I stayed on board and helped to drape them round the ship's rails and top decks. It was probably about ten o'clock when someone mentioned that a reconnaissance plane had been seen in the distance. It worried me, but everyone seemed to be carrying on as before and those in charge said nothing; if they thought it was a friendly plane it was certainly wishful thinking. Sid went ashore about this time to help with the wood-cutting and I continued work on the ship, climbing masts and funnel to place branches of trees in position. We seemed to have used a lot of foliage but still, as midday approached, nobody with half an eye would have mistaken the ship for anything but what she was. I was filthy dirty and everybody else was in the same condition; even the women for once seemed to have forgotten to pay any attention to their appearance. It was also terrifically hot, and being very thirsty and tired I stopped work for a moment to see if I could get a drink. Failing in my efforts to get a drink I made my way to the stern where I had left my suitcase and extracted from it a pair of rubber shoes to replace the leather ones I was wearing. This was a relief to my feet and afterwards proved very lucky. I was wearing besides only a shirt, shorts and a pair of socks. I carried about in the pockets of my shorts, my passport, my wallet containing about $250 (Straits) and my handkerchief, and I also had my steel helmet constantly at hand.

I had just completed changing my shoes when the cry went up "Take cover". We knew that cry only too well, and got down below as quickly as possible. Japanese planes were coming. They made for the abandoned *Kung Wo* first of all and dropped a stick of bombs. She sank within a couple of minutes; then they came at us. Someone said to me, "There are twenty-seven of them almost overhead". We lay down on the greasy, filthy deck of the hold, and a few seconds later the noise of doves in flight was followed by a hit on our ship.

The ship had received a direct hit by a bomb on the bridge, and as I was near the stern the first indication I got of the damage was the noise of steam escaping from broken pipes. This was followed by the crackling of fire, the screams of women, children and wounded.

The planes passed on and we came up from below. The ship was hopelessly on fire. Many had been killed and many wounded. There was no panic, but naturally a good deal of excitement.

There was nothing to do but abandon the ship. The distance to the shore was not great, but still it was probably beyond the ability of most of the passengers to swim to land without assistance. We had now on board a considerable number of wounded: some had come aboard at Singapore, some had been hit while in Singapore harbour, and the rest had received their wounds in this last attack. The supply of lifeboats and rafts was quite inadequate for the crammed ship; there were not many lifebelts, so the obvious thing to do was to throw overboard every piece of timber that could be found to give people something to hold on to. While such life boats as there were were being loaded up with women and wounded I busied myself throwing tables and chairs and all the wood I could find or rip off into the water. Gradually the ship emptied and eventually, finding nothing further to do, I let myself into the water by means of a rope-ladder which was hanging over the side.

Before leaving the ship I noticed that those on the *Tien Kwang* had abandoned her although she had not been hit.

She was much nearer the land than we were, and so her passengers and crew got away comparatively easily, most of them swimming the distance. Many of those, both women and men, who were lucky enough to have lifebelts, decided to put their faith in these rather than wait for places in the boats or rafts which they might not get. They accordingly lowered themselves into the water and made for the shore.

I had no lifebelt or other assistance, but hoped to be able to reach the shore some four hundred yards away. My first sensation on entering the water was a pleasant feeling of coolness and cleanliness. The water was green and calm, and it seemed very restful after the horrors of the ship. Someone shouted: "Take off your helmet", and I was surprised to find I was still wearing it. I placed it upside down on the water and let it float away, it lightened me a little. A number of people were in the water around me and soon I overtook a woman swimming, with a life-jacket, who asked me to stay beside her; she was frightened the planes would come back. I said, "They won't come back", knowing I was lying. We swam together till about half-way across and then we saw the planes almost overhead again returning to the attack.

In this and subsequent attacks I am unable to say whether the Japanese were trying to get the *Tien Kwang* and further damage the *Kuala*, or whether they were trying to get the survivors, but the results were the same. The ships were close together and there were people in the boats near them and in the water; and any bombs dropped on or near the ships were bound to get some of the survivors. As the bombs were falling in the second attack I instinctively submerged completely, which I could not have done if I had had a lifebelt. Whether this saved me I cannot say, but when I rose again the planes had passed on, and the water around seemed less crowded. Under the water I had heard splinters plonk in the sea all around me; they seemed to be very close and numerous, and in fact at the time I thought it was machine-gun fire, but others say there was no machine-gunning. My swimming companion was nowhere to be seen. One bomb had hit the shore at the point I was making for and had landed among some of those who had already got there; the ships were not hit.

I continued swimming and had just about enough energy to reach land. A soldier gave me a hand to get up the sharp rocks out of the water, then we both dived for the jungle as planes were heard again. More bombs fell but nothing came very close to us. Those who had landed at, or near, the same spot as I and who had not already gone ahead were now doing the obvious thing, pushing through the jungle, up the hill and as far from the ships as possible. In my semi-exhausted condition I found it very hard work; the hill was very steep and I could only mount it by catching on to trailers and branches and heaving myself up. Half-way up the planes were coming again, and I made a frantic effort to reach an overhanging piece of rock for cover. I managed this, but just in time, for this was to be my nearest escape from bombs. A bomb fell a few yards away; blast and splinters flew by and parts of the rock I was sheltering under peeled off and fell on my face and eyes. When I got up, the trees around were seared and torn and half-a-dozen soldiers near me had been killed. If this bomb was aimed at the ships it was a bad miss.

Another attack was launched and further bombs were dropped before I reached the top of the hill, but this time they were well away. The Japanese returned at intervals all that day and attacked the *Tien Kwang* again and again, but by the end of the day she had not had a direct hit. This is

Part of the Singapore Docks

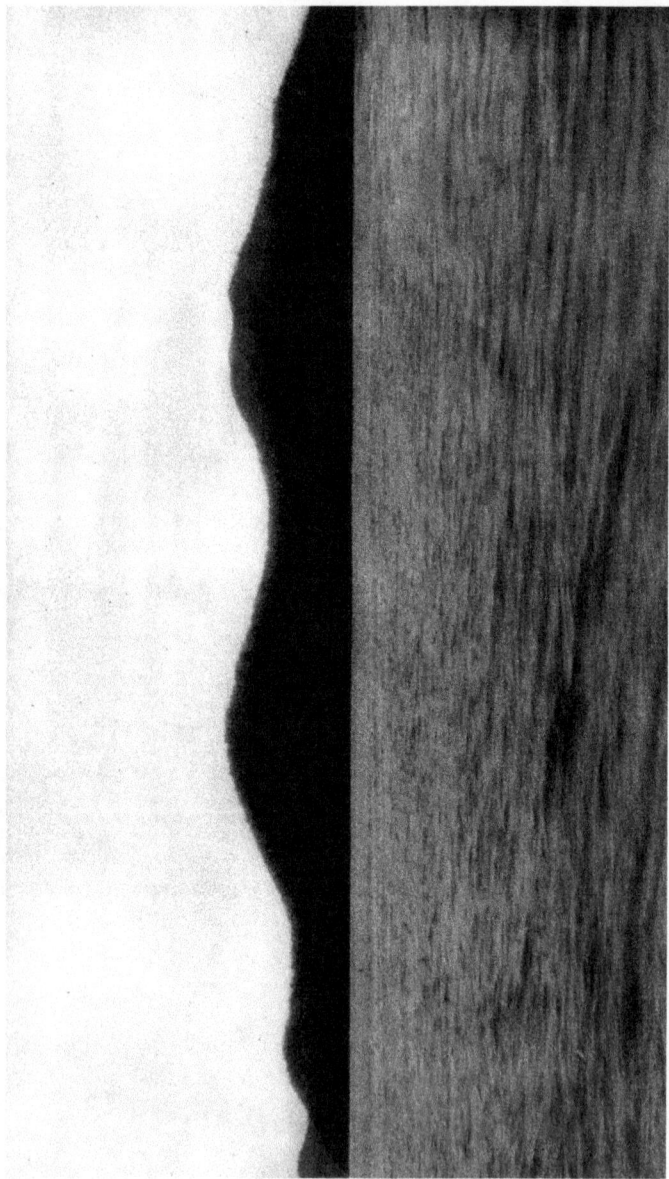

Pompong Looked at from the Sea

really an amazing thing, for the *Kung Wo* and the *Kuala* and other ships which we afterwards heard about were all hit at the first attempt.

The top of the hill, when I reached it, was an astonishing sight. Scattered about everywhere were groups of women dressed only in panties and brassieres, and sometimes not even both of these garments. They had taken off all their other clothes to dry and had hung them up in the patches of sunlight which penetrated the trees. Groups of men there were also, mostly dressed in shorts and shirts and without shoes or stockings. Many had no shirts and some had only under-pants and nothing else.

After a rest to recover from exhaustion there was a general movement down the hill to the side of the island remote from the ships. This was where the short stretch of sand lay, and was afterwards known to everybody as 'Sandy Beach'. This beach was completely covered when the tide was up, but at other times a stretch of about two hundred yards long of clean sand was left. There was about fifty feet of level ground between high-water and the foot of the hill; it was really a continuation of the beach, but was covered with mangrove trees. It formed the site of the camp which was now established. It faced east.

The *Tien Kwang* was a small ship and she probably had not more than two hundred on board. They were all men, mostly services, and, as I have said, they abandoned ship after the first attack and probably all of them got safely on land, though a few may have been killed there. The *Kuala* was much the bigger ship and carried many more, including some two hundred and fifty women and children. The survivors from her made for the shore, some in boats, some on rafts, and some by swimming. In these attempts they were scattered very widely; the majority in boats landed at the little bay opposite the ship where the working parties had been cutting branches earlier in the day. There was a strong current running between the ship and the island, so that other boats were carried round the island towards Sandy Beach or away elsewhere. Most of the rafts were carried away and some of the swimmers. All who managed to land on Pompong were, by the end of the day, gathered roughly into two groups, one at Sandy Beach and one at the above-mentioned bay, which afterwards was called the 'Well'.

There is many a grim story told by those who were carried away from the island and survived. But doubtless there was many an instance of courage, fortitude and self-sacrifice which will never be told. These survivors eventually landed on other islands after various periods in or on the water. Some were as long as thirty hours before reaching land. The strong currents which run around these islands carried many boats, rafts and swimmers to and fro within a short distance of land, but so strong were the currents that in some cases it took the exhausted people many hours before they got ashore.

One raft had twenty-six people on it or hanging to it. They all died or fell off, one by one, until there was a sole survivor. This young man, after twenty-six hours, eventually swam to shore and kept himself alive by climbing a coconut tree and getting some nuts. Mr. Cairns, of Penang—whose wife had been killed on the wharf at Singapore—kept himself and his young son of two years afloat for seven or eight hours before he was picked up by a boat. He told me the child went to sleep lying on a lifebelt in the water. The sea, of course, is warm in this part of the world and cold water was scarcely a factor to be feared. Mr. J.B. Ross, Manager of the Mercantile Bank in Singapore, was seven hours afloat with one arm over a lifebelt and the other on an oar before he was picked up. The boats and rafts picked up many lone swimmers, but there must be many who were never picked up. In fact, I was told by one of the occupants of a raft that it was heart-rending to see swimmers go by whom they could not help either because the raft was already full or because the swimmers and the raft could not get together on account of the currents.

One of the worst features of the whole tragedy is the uncertainty which must surround the fate of many people. It is impossible to say who was on these ships when they left Singapore; no accurate list was kept. It is also impossible to say who was killed by the various bombings and who was drowned. It will take years to clear up, as many of the survivors were later captured by the Japanese and others undoubtedly are still living with natives on various islands of this archipelago. All that can be done in the meantime is to rely on the information given by those who eventually got to freedom—and that is very incomplete.

In addition to the ships I have mentioned there were at least two others which left Singapore the same evening as we did. They were the *Dragonfly* and the *Grasshopper.* Both were attacked about the same time as the *Kuala;* the first stick of bombs sank the *Dragonfly* immediately, and a passenger on the *Grasshopper* who was an eye-witness told me he thought there must have been a seventy-five per cent casualty list. So far as I know both these ships carried only men, Service personnel and a few civilians. The *Grasshopper* was also hit, but the captain managed to run her aground on an island and most of her complement got ashore. These survivors were machine-gunned on the shore and there were many casualties. This all occurred some distance from us and we did not see any of it, but afterwards learned about it when we met the survivors.

I cannot say how many of these small ships left Singapore with evacuees on February 12th and 13th, but I have heard it said that eleven ships were sunk not far from the locality where the *Kuala, Tien Kwang, Kung Wo, Shu Kwang, Dragonfly,* and *Grasshopper* were bombed. I have no means of checking this figure, but it seems a likely one. Again, I cannot say who routed these ships, but it seems reasonable to assume that it was the Naval authorities in Singapore, for they were flying the White Ensign, though that would not be necessary to confirm Admiralty control.

I am reluctant to criticize without full knowledge of the circumstances, but on the face of it the whole of this evacuation seems to have been badly managed. The Naval authorities must have known the dangers from aerial attack. The bombing of the *Kung Wo* and *Shu Kwang*—which took place before the other four sailed-must have warned them, if any warning was necessary, unless their sources of information were very faulty. At that time it was fairly certain that any aerial attack on ships would be made by day, and so to me the obvious thing was to send all these ships over-night straight across to Sumatra, a journey which could easily be made during darkness. The lack of ports on the east coast of Sumatra may have been a deterrent, but it would have been much safer to land the evacuees by small boats at various villages on the coast and up the rivers than to try to get through to Batavia. The ships were mostly of small draught and a close approach even to primitive ports was possible. Batavia was already subject to many air attacks and, as it happened, the Japanese captured Palembang aerodrome on February 15th. The possession of this aerodrome made attacks on the approaches to Batavia very easy. It would, in all probability, have been February 18th or 19th before the ships could reach Batavia even if they had not been sunk prior to that, so the occupation of Palembang certainly made arrival there problematic.

As it was, the ships were evidently told to hide among the islands during the day and travel by night and thus try to make Batavia. Looking back thereon, it seems crazy to think that hiding among the islands was possible. The ships had to lie out at least a few hundred yards and the islands hid them not at all, except perhaps from low-flying aircraft at one or two points of the compass. The ships were packed with men from the Navy, Army, and Air Force, there was a sprinkling of civilian men on each, and on the *Kuala* there was a large number of women and some children. In my opinion these ships-flying White Ensigns and carrying service personnel—were legitimate targets for Japanese bombers. The fact that women and children were on one ship was mismanagement on our part and not proper reason to expect immunity. We did not get it; the Japanese employed upwards of forty aircraft and made a very thorough job of their blitz on last-minute evacuee shipping.

As St. Valentine's Day, 1942, was nearing its close, a state of affairs which defies description prevailed in this section of the Malay Archipelago. Perhaps never before in the long period of recorded history was there anything to compare with it. Men, women, and children in ones and twos, in dozens, in scores, and in hundreds were cast upon these tropical islands within an area of say four hundred square miles. Men and women of many races, of all professions, engineers, doctors, lawyers, businessmen, sisters, nurses, housewives, sailors, soldiers, and airmen, all ship wrecked. Between the islands on the phosphorescent sea floated boats and rafts laden with people; and here and there, upheld by his lifebelt, the lone swimmer was striving to make land. All around the rafts and swimmers were dismembered limbs, dead fish and wreckage drifting with the currents; below, in all probability, were sharks; and above, at intervals, the winged machines of death. Among those who had escaped death from bombs or the sea there was not one who did not suffer from mutilations, wounds, sickness, hunger, cold, dirt, fear, or loss, and none knew what the morrow would bring forth. It was a ghastly tragedy, a catastrophe beyond measure.

CHAPTER EIGHT

POMPONG

MANY YEARS MAY PASS before the fate of all those who intended evacuating in the last days of Singapore will be known for certain. Some there were who came to the wharves, but deciding at the last minute not to take the risk, remained behind. Some were killed on the wharves and some by the bombing in the Singapore Roads.

When the ship was hit lying off Pompong there must have been a good number of deaths especially among the Eurasian and Chinese nurses who were, for the most part, in that quarter of the ship which the bomb hit. Later, there seemed to be very few of them on the island. The sea also took its toll of those who survived these bombings, and finally, when bombs fell on the island itself, still more were killed.

During the few hours that the *Kuala* was intact an attempt was made to list the passengers, but this list was lost with the ship. In any case I never saw or heard of it again. At a rough guess I should say there were about five hundred souls on the *Kuala*, made up of about two hundred and fifty women and children, seventy-five P.W.D. officers, fifty civilian men and one hundred and twenty-five Navy, Army, Air Force and crew. The *Tien Kwang* had probably another two hundred—including civilian men, Navy, Army, Air Force and crew.

A list of those who were on Pompong Island was also compiled, but was probably retained by Group-Captain Nunn and may not be available now. This list showed, if I remember aright, about two hundred women and children, thirty or forty civilian men, and some four hundred Navy, Army, and Air Force.

As I have indicated earlier, these six hundred and forty people were, by the afternoon of the 14th, gathered roughly into two camps-one at Sandy Beach and one at the Well site. The afternoon was punctuated by cries of "Take cover" as the Japanese bombers returned again and again to attack the *Tien Kwang,* as yet unsunk. Every precaution was taken to prevent planes spotting people on the island, as it was impossible to tell whether they contemplated attacking persons or only the still floating ship. No one was allowed on the beach, and clothes could not be hung on trees to dry in case they might give our position away. This was particularly trying, as most of us had nothing but wet clothes and were anxious to get them dried before night fell.

The first activity of many of us was to try to find friends. I had not seen Sid go ashore so was apprehensive of his fate, but someone told me he was all right. It was some hours before we met and I think he had given me up. He had worked his way round the coast to Sandy Beach and, in spite of the previous assurance given me, I was delighted to see him safe.

Squadron-Leader Farwell took charge of the camp at Sandy Beach, and we have much to thank him for. As is inevitable in a show like this he did not please everybody, but he certainly gave positive direction to our efforts and controlled activities in a determined manner. Behind his military manner he had a very kind heart and was most approachable and ready to listen to any proposals.

A review of the situation now showed that we were in a very unenviable position. No wireless message had been sent out, I was told, as the apparatus available on the ships was out of order. We appeared to have no communication with the outside world whatever. Our location was only roughly known and the food and water position was critical. Pompong was by no means the desert island of the story-books, which usually flows with milk and honey. It was a most unfriendly island, nearly all hill and covered with thick jungle which was exceedingly difficult to make one's way through. Apart from the short stretch of sand at Sandy Beach the coast was jagged rocks and round slippery boulders. There was not even a coconut tree on the island- nothing edible whatsoever. Fortunately there was one well situated at Well Site camp to which it gave the name, but we did not know this until later.

A few beakers of water had been taken from the lifeboats and also some biscuits, tinned meat, and fish. These were all the provisions at Sandy Beach and there were several hundred people to provide for. Well Site camp was very similarly placed, except that the well there promised a limited, but enduring, source of water.

Captain Briggs, master of the *Tien Kwang*, was at Sandy Beach, and it was decided that, when darkness was falling and it was reasonably safe, he should go on board his ship— if she was still afloat—with what members of his crew he could find, and try to get her going. It was known that she was damaged, but he thought that he might be able to make the east coast of Sumatra taking the crew only, and there endeavour to get assistance. There was one other chance of making contact, for it was expected that the launch, which had visited the *Kuala* that morning and gone off again, had survived and would appear off the island at dusk.

During the course of the afternoon a Camp Headquarters was established and all that was possible was done for the wounded. It was extremely fortunate that some medical supplies were got off the lifeboats and also that among the survivors there were some doctors and a number of sisters and nurses. During the days and weeks that followed these men and women proved invaluable. The very highest praise is due to them for the way in which they carried out the tasks of healing with meagre supplies, but with infinite patience and skill, in the most unusual and unhelpful conditions.

Stretchers were made with branches hewn from the jungle and rough pieces of sail and hessian. The healthy gave clothes to the wounded, and all types of medical and surgical attention was rendered even to the extent of an amputation. Some beyond medical aid died, but the great majority of the injured—when they eventually got away—had hope of recovery largely due to the doctors, sisters, and nurses who tended them so assiduously. When it was nearly dusk the launch we had hoped for returned. Squadron-Leader Farwell informed her of our situation, and it was arranged that she should try to get to Sumatra and obtain assistance for us. She had to take survivors from the *Kung Wo* and *Shu Kwang,* but agreed to take some half-dozen of our worst stretcher-cases. It was a tough job getting them aboard, as she was lying some distance out from the strand and it was necessary to carry the wounded shoulder-high through water to reach her. Some of us got wet through again in this operation.

Meantime, the captain of the *Tien Kwang* had got together some of his crew and had gone off to his ship. He found that while the ship was still afloat she was badly damaged and leaking. He might have been able to get her going if sufficient crew had been found, but apparently he was unable to muster enough bands willing to attempt the voyage, and, in the circumstances, he loaded two boats with blankets, medical stores for the wounded, and provisions. He then, I was told, assisted his ship to sink, which she did before morning. This, I believe, was done so that the bombers might let us alone, but to me it seemed like throwing away one of our precious chances. The boats which had been loaded were not, on account of the darkness and currents, able to return to Sandy Beach and so had to be run ashore about half-way back. The crew carried the blankets back to the camp for the use of the wounded, but the provisions were left until the next morning.

With this unpleasant news in our ears we tried to settle down to pass the night, each person selecting the spot which he thought the most comfortable. This night was to be the most dreadful I had ever spent. Sid and I had had no food all day except the scanty meal in the early morning. We had not had anything to drink either until just before dark when half a cup of water was issued to each person. Our clothes were wet and we were filthy dirty, but our greatest misery was the cold wind which now started to blow. Facing east, as we were, we got the full force of the monsoon which, on account of our wet condition and the fact that we had been long resident in the tropics, seemed icy. We had, of course, no cover except the trees, and we lay on the damp sand behind the beach. After an hour or so we rose from our first position to search for a more sheltered spot, but in the darkness tripped over tree-roots and other people every step so that we soon gave it up and returned to near the Camp Headquarters and found another place no better than the first.

That night we lay with arms around each other trying to

reduce the terrible cold. I heard groans a few yards away and was able to pick out the figure of a man sitting in a crouching position at the base of a tree. The poor fellow had nothing on whatever except the briefest of brief slips. He was shaking all over with cold. I called him to come beside us, which he did, and we three lay as close as it was possible to do. He was a very young soldier of magnificent build and it was distressing to witness his young flesh shivering in the icy wind. Apart from the cold it was impossible to get anything like comfortable on the uneven sand with roots through it and no pillow, and I well remember Sid's agonized cry of "Oh, my God!" in the middle of the night. Just before daylight the rising tide forced some people to move their 'beds' back farther from the sea and necessitated hauling up a boat which had previously been on dry beach. Sid and I got up to lend a hand with this, and so a night of unforgettable misery ended. We never saw, or at least never recognized, our soldier bed-fellow again.

Volunteers were called for to go back along the rocky shore and bring the stores which Captain Briggs had deposited the night before. I went with the party and was bending down to pick up some tins when a fit of giddiness attacked me and I stumbled and fell. It was only momentary, however, and I was quickly on my feet again. I attributed it, at the time, to lack of food, but this momentary giddiness assailed me at intervals for the next few months, even after I was getting regular meals, and I now think it must have been one of the peculiar effects of blast.

When all the provisions and water had been collected at Camp Headquarters it was obvious that very strict rationing would have to be resorted to, as there was no telling how long we would be on the island or, indeed, if we would ever get off it. We started with two meals a day, each consisting of a pound tin of bully beef between six and about half a ship's biscuit per person. We had about half a cup of water three times a day.

On this first morning Sid and I were ravenously hungry, but more even than food we desired water. At that time we scarcely knew of the existence of the Well Site Camp, but we heard rumours of a well being somewhere on the island, in fact the captain of the launch which called the night before had said he knew that such a well existed. As there was nothing to do we started out with the intention of finding this well, situated we believed on the other side. With the high tide it was not possible to go round the shore, so up over the hill we went—in our condition a most exhausting business.

Japanese planes came over several times that morning, possibly to search for the *Tien Kwang* or to satisfy themselves that no more ships were 'hiding' among the islands. I noticed a small launch several miles out at sea; from where it had come, or what it was I could not know, but one bomb was dropped near it. So far as I could see it escaped injury and was not again attacked. No bombs were dropped on the island itself after the 14th, but until I left the Japanese sent at least one plane over every day and probably knew much of what was happening.

At the top of the hill we met a party bringing in a badly wounded man whom they had found in the jungle, so from then on we searched for wounded and kept a sharp look-out for any such cases. We did not find any, but we saw bodies, including those who had been killed by the bomb which had so nearly finished me the previous day. I am afraid these men were never buried. The lack of food and the conditions of living made everyone so weak that all

85

unessential work had to be cut out. It was impossible to bury men on the hill as the ground was very hard and there were no tools to dig with. The task of bringing the dead down to Sandy Beach was too much for exhausted men, and most of the corpses were a long way from the camp. Graves in the sand were scooped out for those who had died near Sandy Beach and for bodies and limbs which were washed up, but beyond that burial was impossible. It seems callous, but all available energies had to be utilized in tasks for the living.

Those who do not know Malayan jungle would be surprised how very difficult it is to find one's way, even on a small island like this one. One can see nothing but the immediate jungle, and the sea might be only a few yards away without one knowing it. Before long we had only the vaguest idea what part of the island we were at. We knew, of course, that if we went down a hill at any point we would eventually get to the shore, but at what point it was impossible to tell. Airmen in Malaya are told that if they land in the jungle and get away with it, they must always walk downhill. It is no good waiting to be found, it might take months or eternity. If one is able to achieve a continuous downhill course, then eventually a river will be found and ultimately the sea. Or, if one is lucky, a village on the river-bank before that. In my pleasure-flying before the war I had frequently piloted a machine over the green carpet of undergrowth and jungle which covers unending miles of the Malayan peninsula, and I had never lost my dread of a forced landing in its leafy fastnesses. I dreaded not so much the possibility of a crash and a sudden ending as the more gruesome possibility of being uninjured and wandering for days in tractless jungle till slow starvation finished it. Men have been known to leave the road with the intention of going only a few yards into the trees and have taken days to get out or have not come out at all.

There was, of course, no chance of such a fate on this island, but it was impossible to say at what point we should descend to the sea in order to have a chance of striking the Well. We decided at last to go down what seemed to be a dried watercourse. It was just as hard to descend this hill as it was to climb it, and at the bottom we were exhausted and terribly thirsty.

On first sight there was nothing but unfriendly rock and we felt foolish and filled with despair. We had added to our thirst and found no water, and we had no stomach for further effort. Luckily, on a second look, I saw a damp rock about ten feet away and a depression about the size of a small saucer at the foot of it. This was filled with water seeping down the rock and a trial showed me that it was fresh. With joy I threw myself on my stomach and lapped up its contents. It took about a minute to fill up again. We drank and drank from it for a long time and seldom has water been more welcome. As we were resting afterwards Captain Briggs and two others joined us. They had followed the same dry watercourse in the hope of a drink. They were thoroughly exhausted and asked us in spent voices if we had a drink. The trickle of water was truly a God-send.

We were almost opposite the point where the *Tien Kwang* had sunk and the sea was covered with oil. Having recovered slightly we noticed a kit-bag floating among some debris and got our first coat of oil in securing it. Oil was to add considerably to our miseries during the time we were on the island, for before long all the rocks on the beach were covered with it. Every time we went to the shore we got covered in it, so that we could not use the sea even for cleaning ourselves, and the film on the rocks made getting about on the shore extremely hazardous. Many a sharp cut and nasty bruise was caused by slipping on oil.

We had to rip open the kit-bag, where we found a blanket, a ground-sheet, a shirt, a pair of shorts, a steel helmet and—joy of joys—a small emergency ration of chocolate. This latter gave us a small piece each, but it sufficed to put new spirit into us, and as the others did not want the clothes Sid and I started back to the camp laden with them. We had now a spare shirt and a pair of shorts between us and a steel helmet each, and this was the beginning of a most extraordinary assortment of odds and ends which we subsequently collected. The blanket and ground-sheet would have to go the 'hospital'—as the patch of ground where the wounded were lying was called—but first of all they would require drying, for they were covered with oil and soaking wet. At Sandy Beach we hung everything up to dry at the spot where we intended to sleep that night.

Sid and I discussed the situation and its possibilities. He opened the conversation with: "How long do you think we should give it before throwing ourselves into the sea?" Sid was a realist and turned a mathematical mind on to all problems. He liked to look thoroughly at all the known data and draw from them a logical conclusion. If there were two possible conclusions he always stated the least favourable one, so that if something better turned up then we were at least to the good. I held we had a fair chance, for the launch which had called the night before might get through, and failing that we might contact a passing ship or native craft. In my optimism I was sure that the launch, if it got through, would succeed in sending early naval assistance, for I thought that the authorities could not allow a large number of people—including women—to remain on these islands until they starved. The Navy, however, must have been otherwise engaged, for so far as I know neither then nor at any other time was Naval assistance given in rescuing these stranded people from the Islands. This was the day that Singapore fell and Palembang was occupied, and had I known this I should have been even less hopeful. We had, of course, expected Singapore to fall, but we did not expect the Japanese immediately to establish themselves south of us as well as north.

In the afternoon we saw a row-boat, obviously a ship's boat, about two or three miles away and apparently trying to make our island. It struggled for hours, but could not do it. It moved north and south but never got any nearer. The currents were too strong that afternoon, but trying again through the night it reached us at dawn the next morning.

I talked to many men and women before dark that evening and tried to gather the general attitude to our plight. On the whole I was discouraged by these conversations. I found among the women a blind faith that we would be rescued, but it was not based on any good reasoning; the men were largely apathetic and offered few constructive thoughts or proposals. This attitude was distressingly general among those of all professions who were evacuees or refugees from Malaya and whom I met on this and other islands. It may have been that they had gone through so much since the start of the war, and especially in the last days of Singapore, that they were numbed and the fight had gone out of them. The zest for life and freedom and the will to work their own salvation was sadly lacking. It was often difficult to get volunteers for any job that had to be done, and they were content to leave their fate in the hands of the few who could bestir themselves. There was, however, a very laudable spirit of helpfulness between individual and individual, and all seemed to share with utter unselfishness any small comforts or assets which they had.

One striking example of this unselfishness was the way that friends of the wounded would bend over the disabled persons when planes came overhead to protect the latter with their own bodies from any flying splinters or blast which might come that way.

There was no news of any possible rescue that day or of any further steps being taken to obtain help. No craft other than the one I have mentioned was seen.

Sid and I found a more sheltered nook that night, but it was still very cold, so much so that we decided that the blanket—wet as it was—would be better than nothing, and we covered ourselves with that and so obtained a reasonable amount of sleep. Daylight here ended about 7 p.m. and there was twelve hours darkness. Nothing could be done after dark so that we all lay for twelve hours in our 'beds' at night and usually several hours during the day. Indeed, everybody grew very weak from lack of food, and the slightest exertion caused a disproportionate amount of exhaustion.

On the following morning, February 16th, the boat which had been trying to get to us the evening before managed to arrive. It contained Mr. S. A. Jordan, Mr. D. J. Davies, Mr. P. O'Connell, and others, and had come from one of the other islands possibly ten miles away to tell us that there were thirty-five people there with no provisions whatever. One of our available boats in consequence manned with volunteers and supplied with some food and water from our scanty store was despatched to the island. It never returned. We subsequently heard that the people on the island had been picked up by a Chinese tongkang, and our boat, finding nobody, went on with its relief crew to another inhabited island and joined some others there. Fearing the safety of the first boat a second was despatched from Pompong, but it returned having failed to find out anything.

It was now obvious that Sandy Beach could not be used much longer as a camp on account of the shortage of water, and it was decided that everyone except the badly wounded and a few attendants should be transferred to Well Site Camp. During the morning this was accomplished, but it was a difficult and exhausting climb and descent for some.

Sandy Beach was quite picturesque; the beach was pleasant and there was at least a narrow strip of comparatively level ground. Well Site was, on the other hand, the most depressing place imaginable. There was no level ground and the trees went right to the water's edge. The ground was covered with a fine brown dust which clung to everything; and the shore, when the tide was down, was strewn with large round slippery boulders where there was any break in the jagged rocks. Both rocks and boulders were covered with oil.

This was my first visit to Well Site, and there I found many people I did not know were on the island. All were filthy dirty and more or less depressed. The situation of this camp was so horrible that under the best circumstances no one could feel cheerful there. The food question was serious and we were divided into parties of twelve for rations. There were two 'meals' a day, and a party got a pound tin of bully beef and six biscuits at a meal, so that each person had one-twelfth of a tin of bully and half a biscuit. This ration was practically unchanged until we left the island, except that later the half-biscuit was replaced by a spoonful of rice. We were able to get about half a mug of water three times a day, which was an improvement on the supply at Sandy Beach.

A few cigarettes had come from somewhere, and so, for those who smoked, Lady Nicotine afforded comfort to the extent of one cigarette a meal. These meals were eaten under the filthiest conditions. The food had to be held in the hand or on a dirty leaf and eaten with the fingers. As one's hands could not be washed the whole procedure was anything but hygienic.

The appearance of our colony was amusing if tragic. Men and women were dressed in all sorts of rags, and the men's beards were getting longer and longer. Many had no footwear, and to those with tender feet this was a sore problem. Mr. A. C. Potts, who got ashore with long trousers, converted them into shorts, used the balance to wrap his feet in and lashed those wrappings with trailers from the jungle. This was but an example of the devices resorted to, but how the women solved many clothing difficulties I do not know. Most of the men were without shirts, and it was obvious that some of them had gallantly bequeathed theirs to the fair sex. The most picturesque citizen of Pompong was, I think, Mr. R. A. Stewart, Manager of the Hong Kong and Shanghai Bank in Singapore. His hair and beard were reminiscent of a Biblical figure, and the delusion was enhanced by a bare body and a pair of trousers with one leg long and one rolled to the knee. In addition, he always carried a long staff and looked a veritable sage. Almost everybody had wounds, cuts, or bruises, and this patched-up humanity—covered with brown dust and oil—looked far from attractive and must have made Raffles Hotel and Tanglin Club turn in their graves, so to speak.

Among the few who were not content to let things drift were Messrs. Morgan and Mitford of the P.W.D. They proposed to take a boat and go out into the blue and look for help. Group Captain Nunn, who was in charge of Well Site, agreed, and with others they prepared a boat and sail. I should have liked to join this effort, but the thing was all arranged before I knew. They started off in the afternoon before dark and carried with them many of our hopes. Whether or not their journey was of any use to us I cannot say, for I never heard of any assistance which was directly attributed to them, but doubtless they spread the news of our plight. They eventually got to safety by much the same route as we afterwards essayed.

When this boat was starting off we saw a Chinese junk approaching at a considerable distance. The boat made straight for the junk and had some talk with her. What was said I do not know, but the junk continued to approach Pompong, and just as we were sure that this was the beginning of help she sailed by at several hundred yards distance. All our shouts did not bring any response, and our hopes were dashed to the ground.

This action on the part of the junk was our first taste of the general unfriendliness of the ordinary native towards us. This unfriendliness was largely, I think, based on fear. The white man's star was setting in the East, temporarily at any rate, and the natives feared that the Japanese would take revenge on them for any aid they rendered us. There were very notable exceptions to this, but still it was the general feeling.

We had now two lifeboats and a dinghy left at the island and over six hundred people. It was impossible to think of taking them away on these three boats even by relays. Group-Captain Nunn said that the order of evacuation must be first, women and children and wounded, then civilians, then the P.W.D. Unit, and lastly the Services. This, he said, was the normal procedure for evacuating any place.

Some Service Units who had received instructions in Singapore to go as quickly as possible to other jobs were not very pleased with this arrangement. As it happened it was never necessary to adhere strictly to the order.

That night, Monday, February 17th, it was considered likely that a ship or ships would arrive, as there had been time for the launch which had visited us the first night to reach Sumatra and for assistance to get to us. A crew was detailed for the dinghy and told they might be required any time during the night, and watches were set along the shore to pick up any craft that might come near.

Sid and I had made our new home in a hollow near the water's edge. It was quite a promising-looking place apart from the fact that roots stuck up every few inches. Nowhere else we could find was any better, so we passed it off by saying that as the equator perhaps passed right through the island it was bound to stick up in places.

Fortunately this side of the island was much warmer than Sandy Beach, for our blanket and ground-sheet were now in the hospital. It will always remain a mystery to me how, in spite of wettings and exposure, none of these people seemed to catch cold. Apart from one man who caught a severe chill I did not hear either then, or subsequently, of any case of cold, chill or pneumonia. In the warmer atmosphere of Well Site we slept the sleep of the exhausted and only woke up when the 'equator' seemed to make greater dents than usual in our bodies or when the jungle rustled nearby. Some said these rustlings were caused by rats, some said by snakes, but whichever is true they made unpleasant interludes in the night's repose.

As darkness fell about 7 p.m. everyone lay down at that hour and remained in his sleeping-place till daylight appeared some twelve hours later. On this first night at Well

Site, Sid and I were wakened by the watch on the shore hailing a craft at sea. A few minutes later a cry went up for the dinghy crew to turn out. This cry was repeated several times, and did not seem to meet with any response, so Sid rushed through the bushes to see if he could do anything. In these early days Sid had an amazing amount of energy and was always the first to assist in any useful work; his restless mind urged to its limits a body not at all used to this kind of existence. Now he and Mr. Pape accomplished the task of taking the dinghy out to the craft which had arrived off the island, a task made very difficult by the nature of the rocks on the shore and the black darkness which obscured everything.

The boat which had come to our assistance was the *Tanjong Pinang*, a little launch of sixty-seven tons which had been informed of our plight by those who had visited us in the small launch the first night we were on the island. The *Tanjong Pinang* was prepared to take off as many as she could, and a cry went up for all the women and children to get ready to embark.

From all parts of the dark jungle they came in high spirits. This was rescue from appalling conditions. This was the route to freedom. The embarkation of about one hundred and seventy women, some children, and a few badly wounded men proved extremely difficult. The only suitable place for entering the little row-boat which was to take them to the launch was one hundred yards along the shore from the spot where the beaten path met the rocks. This distance was for half its length covered with large round slippery boulders coated with oil, and for the other half with sharp jagged rocks. The men formed a chain from jungle to row-boat and passed the women and wounded along as best they could, receiving many nasty cuts and bruises in the process. One or two torches were available, but these could only be used sparingly owing to our fear of detection, so for the most part the embarkation was carried on by sound and feel.

I well remember the hopefulness of these women, and many of the cheerful and encouraging little things they said to us as they passed along the chain. One woman said: "You men are wonderful the way you help us, we couldn't do without you"; and I thought, well, if there is anybody to be praised for their work on this island it is the women doctors, sisters, and nurses. Another said: "You will follow soon and we'll see you shortly"; and still another, as she handed a small torch to me and her raincoat to my neighbour: "We mustn't take away anything which might be of use to you who are left."

Some women with hospital experience volunteered to stay behind and look after the wounded who were left, and so they remained. Mrs. R. L. Nunn got down as far as the embarkation spot and then asked me to find her husband for her. He came along in a few minutes and she said to him: "Rex, I don't want to go if you are not coming." She evidently persuaded him to allow her to stay, for she did not leave the island until she was able to accompany him.

It was three in the morning before all were on board and the launch with its precious cargo pushed off to a fate which up to the time of writing is not yet certain. Certain it is that the launch has not turned up at any British, allied, or neutral port, and months after she had left us we were convinced that she had been sunk; but the latest information seems to indicate that she was captured by the Japanese somewhere in the Java Sea. Capture is better than sinking, or so we hope, but in any case it is a tragedy of the first magnitude.

Sunlight on the Malayan Jungle

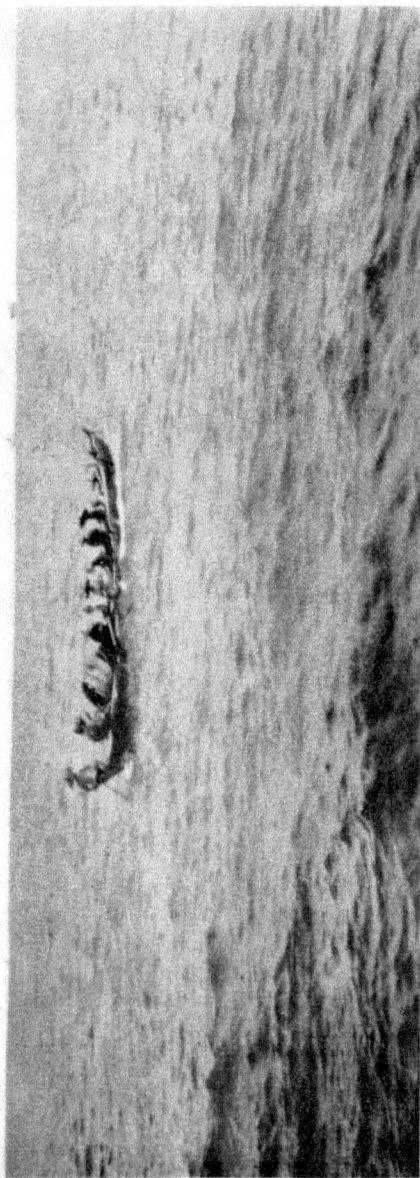

A Sampan with its Load

While I had been helping with the embarkation Sid had been working with the dinghy and talking to the captain of the *Tanjong Pinang*. I met him before I returned to my resting-place and he was wet through by his exertions with the dinghy in a choppy sea. He produced from his salt-water-soaked pocket a small handful of dried figs which the captain had given him, and we ate them with great relish only to feel hungrier afterwards. He told me that the launch was going to try and make Batavia, which he thought was extremely foolish, as it would be much safer to go straight to Sumatra overnight and be in comparative safety by morning or at least close to the mainland. Sid was more right than he knew about this, because Singapore had fallen almost thirty-six hours previously and the Japanese had also established themselves in Palembang in the south of Sumatra, thus barring the route to Batavia. The captain did not know this at the time; in fact, he thought Singapore was still holding, but even if that had been true the course he proposed seemed to be a perilous one.

When the ship had gone I returned to my sleeping-place; but Sid, being wet through, made his way to the 'hospital', where he was able to get a blanket as so many of the wounded were now gone. Stripping himself of all his clothes he curled up in the blanket and went to sleep where he was. This blanket remained in our possession and was a great comfort in the many and varied sleeping-places we afterwards adorned.

The next day, our fourth on the island, had very little to mark its passing. We had high hopes that another ship would come along to supplement the first, but the day and night passed and our only visitors were a very small Malay *koleh* in the late afternoon—which I think came out of curiosity—and a sampan at night. The sampan brought a little food, but still more welcome was the news which it brought that an effort was being made to get some large Chinese tongkangs or junks to take the main body off. The sampan departed in a short time, taking with it about five people who were beginning to suffer badly from the privations of the island.

The morning of Wednesday, February 18th, found us in a very dispirited mood. Our miserable lot and the nebulous hopes of rescue were getting us down. Beards were at the very uncomfortable stage, and all our bodies were covered with a thick coating of oil and dirt. We hung around in small groups, and almost all the talk was of the possibility of getting away from Pompong. We knew this would not end our troubles, but whether for better or for worse we wanted desperately to get off that miserable island. I cannot say that hunger troubled us much after the first twenty four hours; true, we had always a craving for food, but I at least did not and I don't think the others felt any acute pains from hunger. Thirst was a different matter and we were all terribly thirsty. When the water ration was being given out we stood in long queues with tongues almost hanging out to get our half-mug of water. Six hundred of us drank from three mugs and a few empty bully tins, some gulping it down, and some sipping it slowly to the intense irritation of the fellow following. When it was finished we retired, counting the hours till the next issue.

I can remember very little of the conversation on the island; in fact, there was very little conversation, people sat in silence for the most part or slept. We were terribly weak. The dead were seldom or never mentioned, events in Singapore before the end were occasionally spoken of, but the greater part of any talk there was was about our present plight and the immediate scanty hopes of rescue. As was perhaps natural in the circumstances there was a deal of dissatisfaction and the team spirit was not very marked. Individual members of groups were loyal to each other, but certain groups were very critical of those who had taken charge. The latter were accused of lack of initiative in planning our departure and of consuming too large a share of the available stores and water. I doubt if there was any truth in these accusations, but men were hungry, thirsty, dirty, uncomfortable, and in despair, and dissatisfaction was easy to foment.

In some ways we were very fortunate. The existence of the well probably saved all our lives, and connected with this was the absence of rain. It is seldom that a week passes in these regions without a shower of rain at least, but we had none that week. If it had rained the well would have been filled with mud and dirt which water rushing down the steep slopes would have been sure to deposit in it—and a heavy shower would possibly have broken down the sides and allowed the tide in, for it was scarcely above high-tide level and, as it was, it had to be bunded off. We were fortunate again that there were no mosquitoes on the island, for of course we had no protection from these deadly insects.

Up to this time it had been deemed unwise to light any fires, but now the ships' biscuits had run out and we had to fall back on rice, which the sampan had brought the night before, so the risk of a fire had to be taken, and one was built under careful supervision to cook the rice. Japanese planes were over every day, generally in the morning, and when the dreaded sound was heard we took what cover there was behind trees and waited till they passed. We were very careful not to show any signs of habitation; clothes and people were kept well out of the way, and movement and the rustling of the branches was strictly forbidden. One could not help reflecting how one or two planes overhead were able to keep hundreds of people below in a state of terror. Such is the power of modern war machines.

One of these planes came over just after midday on this day and, as luck would have it, a small motor-trawler was approaching the island at the same time. This boat was coming to our aid, sent, I believe, by the Dutch Government, and we cursed the chance which brought it at the same time as the plane. It seemed to us then that this was going to be another disaster, the boat would be sunk and we would be discovered. However, the plane passed over twice and then went off; the miraculous had happened. Looking back now it seems to have been the Japanese policy to leave small craft alone, possibly because these were almost always the property of Asiatics and probably engaged in fishing or native commerce. The Japanese did not wish to antagonize the local population unnecessarily and, after all, these were small fry. Many owe their lives to this policy, for in these and subsequent days many hundreds travelled in small boats and by keeping hidden when the planes were overhead escaped destruction.

This second ship of any size to come to Pompong was loaded up with almost all the remaining women and a number of wounded, and although it sailed away in daylight from the island it crossed the open sea to Sumatra by night and its passengers eventually reached safety. This boat had promised to come back if it got through and, in fact, did so two days later.

We had still some four hundred people on the island, which included only about half a dozen women. We settled down to another period of waiting. Things looked pretty hopeless, as this boat by itself, even if it returned, could never take all of us off before our provisions were exhausted and in time to do any good. It could only take some fifty at a time. The arrival of the promised Chinese junks was, of course, still possible, but we did not place too much faith in this. The boat had brought news which did nothing to ease our minds. Singapore had fallen on Sunday, February 15th, and the Japanese had occupied Palembang on the same day. The battle for Java had also commenced. This all meant that the enemy were in control of the territory north and south of us, and undoubtedly their ships were patrolling the seas between as their aircraft were patrolling the skies. What hope was there?

Our information was of the scantiest, but it began to be apparent that the only possible line of escape would be across Sumatra, through the centre of that large island. It had been known for some time that the Japanese had virtually control of the north part of Sumatra, and now we had received information that they had captured the south. What of the centre? Well, it might be just possible to get across the centre if we were quick, but speed was obviously indicated and there did not seem any means of achieving it.

I had been to Sumatra, but only the northern part of it, and I had no first-hand knowledge of the country south of Medan. Everyone knew, however, that it was a vast island little developed, containing tremendous areas of trackless jungle pierced by some long rivers. There were no ports on the east coast worth mention except Belawan Deli, the port of Medan, but on the west there were one or two such as Bencoolen and Padang. The centre of the country which was, so to speak, opposite where we were, was particularly undeveloped, and of course this might or might not be to our advantage. It was less likely to be quickly overrun by the Japanese; but, on the other hand, it would in all probability take us much longer to cross it, if we ever got there. Meantime, how to get there was the question.

Such thoughts ran through Sid's mind and mine as the trawler faded on the horizon. We were especially worried by the necessity for speed and the lack of any means of achieving it. We decided to go off on any kind of craft, or anything that floated, if we got the chance and it was not required by others. One can only do what seems best at the moment and very often that proves wrong in the long run. So it was with us, for if we had only stayed a little longer than we did we might have got quickly to safety.

As it was we got a chance sooner than we expected, for just before dark a Malay *prahoe* arrived at our island bringing a few bananas and a dirty bag of sago as a gift from the headman of some village or other. In the circumstances it was a generous gift, for all the villages were very short of food as the distribution system had broken down. We had a long talk with the Serang of this boat and learned from him a lot about the distribution of the islands and which of them were inhabited. He also told us about people who had been shipwrecked on other islands and how numbers of them had conjugated at certain places.

As the *prahoe* was about to push off we finally decided to go in it, and spoke to Group-Captain Nunn about it. We told him that if no one else wanted to go we would like to take our chance with this craft. He had no objection, as no one else seemed to fancy it, but he said that he expected the junks to come and the trawler to return soon and everyone would then get away. We, however, preferred a bird in the hand and, putting our few belongings in the blanket, boarded the *prahoe*.

We were just pushing off when a shout went up from the shore and a number of men rushed down to us. They were

Mr. Sturt, Mr. Scott-Ram, Mr. Robertson—all of the Asiatic Petroleum Company—Mr. Samuels, a lawyer from Penang, and Mr. Stocks. They wished to come with us, so we got them into the boat and started our journey to a rather dubious destination.

CHAPTER NINE

SINAJANG

THERE WERE THREE MALAY HANDS besides the old Serang, and these three men started to row as Malays will row in such a boat, that is, by standing facing the bow of the boat and pushing the oars instead of pulling them. For nearly two hours they kept it up and then, when Pompong had fallen behind and the moon was rising, they raised a sail. The Serang said to me: "Pompong sudah hilang, Tuan (Pompong is lost, master)"; and I replied: "Grand; I never wish to see it again."

We had settled down in the bottom of the boat and were carrying on an animated conversation. It was the first cheery talk I had heard since we left Singapore; the sensation of being on the move, of making an effort to reach liberty, had cheered us all up. It was a beautiful night and in a small boat like this it was very unlikely that we should be seen. As the conversation and witticisms became exhausted we started to doze. It was possibly about three or four in the morning when we all awoke; the boat was stationary, the wind had fallen to practically nothing. For a while our crew essayed rowing, but the current was against them and they gave it up. We were so anxious, however, to get somewhere before daylight that we all took turns at the unaccustomed oars and did the best we could in our very weak condition. I doubt if it had much effect, but we kept at it, rowing when we could and resting when we couldn't, until daylight appeared.

Daylight brought the wind and we sailed merrily for a bit. Most of our course was between islands, and early in the morning we saw a few huts on one of them, so we went towards it and landed near a small store which the Serang knew. We dug out the owner and asked what he had to sell. It was little enough in all conscience, but we were able to get a few biscuits and two tins of locally canned pineapple, and this, to us, was a feast. When the meal was over and we had started again I was about to throw one of the empty tins overboard when the Serang intervened and took the tin. I thought he wanted it for drinking purposes, but later, when I unthinkingly threw the other tin over, he made an exclamation of distress and, turning to the sea and skies, he said in a beseeching voice: "Tidapa, dia tida tahoe adat (never mind, he does not know the custom)." It was apparently inviting the wrath of the elements to throw tins overboard.

About eleven o'clock that morning we came to a sizable village called Sinajang, on a proper tropical island covered with coconut palms and girdled with sandy beaches.

This island was not very large, possibly a mile long by about a quarter of a mile wide. The village was on the east side and a very pleasant beach ran most of the length of the west side. There must have been at least three hundred natives living here, and they supported themselves mostly by fishing and growing coconuts. Coconut palms covered almost all of the island, but there were also signs of other products in a small way. A few pineapple plants, some banana trees, fowl, and pigs, but not much of anything except coconuts. The pineapples and bananas did not seem to have any fruit, and the fowl and pigs looked unhealthy but were not constipated to judge from the streets. Some produce evidently came from another island across a narrow intervening strait, which one could see had a certain amount of cultivation but only one or two huts. The village had a main street and there were a few shops on either side. This street was paved with dust. Access to other parts of the island was obtained by paths which had started out to be narrow roads but were sadly neglected and over grown. The shops and houses were of wood with atap roofs, but an odd house with pretensions was on brick stilts and might have a roof of corrugated iron.

At one end of the village was the well and public wash-house. The well water, in our opinion, needed boiling before consumption, but the washing water needed no preparation, and once on the island we quickly found a use for it—not having washed for a week. This water was really quite clean, but almost any water would have made a vast improvement on our bodies and clothes. Immediately opposite the public bath-house was the public latrine, conveniently situated over the sea and consisting of a hut with a door on one side and a hole in the floor.

We landed at the bamboo pier and were met by one or two of the island's visitors, shipwrecks like ourselves. We learnt that there was quite a little colony of them here, gathered from the various ships which had been victims of the blitz on February 14th. There must have been about seventy in all, and Messrs. Ivor Salmond and O'Grady had taken on guidance of the party. We were immediately guided to the village coffee-shop and given a cup, which was nectar. The surroundings and the cups were filthy, but the coffee was not bad and there was lots of sugar. New life flowed through our veins and at that moment we thought of Sinajang as a paradise.

From the village coffee-shop we proceeded to the headquarters of the refugees. A two-story building, if you please, allotted to them by the Amir. The Amir-the Dutch Government's representative in the village-was an educated Malay and seemed to possess almost dictatorial powers on the island. He had been instructed by the Netherlands Indies Government to assist us with food and housing, and this he did to the utmost of his ability. Any expense was, I believe, charged to his Government in the first place in the hope of subsequently recovering it from the Malayan Governments. Needless to say the food and housing left a great deal to be desired, but it wasn't the Amir's fault: good accommodation did not exist on the island and neither did the sort of food we usually live on.

The food supplied to us was, in fact, rice and more rice, but there was usually a tin of bully beef or some fish or vegetables to flavour it with, and on one memorable occasion a pumpkin. We had it twice a day—at 10 a.m. and 5 p.m. One could supplement these meals now and then with purchases made in the local shops, but the buying of food was discouraged, and indeed there was practically nothing to buy beyond a few bananas, a coconut, and a very small ration of bread if one was there at the right time. The price of everything was exorbitant. The inhabitants did not want us there; our presence was likely to draw the enemy, who would take revenge for any assistance they rendered us; and then, of course, we increased the island's consumption of food by a large percentage. In the meantime, stocks were running out and no more were coming in. These people normally carry on trade mainly with Singapore, and although the islands are Dutch it is Straits currency which is used. No supplies had come from Singapore for some time, so while the islanders might eke out a bare existence on local products they certainly could not feed for long the best part of a hundred visitors. No wonder then that they did not look with favour on our presence, but somehow it came as a shock to us who knew the Malay and Chinaman in peace-time, how friendly they were, how ready to help, how anxious to sell their wares. Things had indeed changed; now they were reluctant to sell anything from their scanty stocks and, if persuaded to do so, charged scandalous prices which we in our turn—those of us who had any money—were reluctant to pay, for we did not know where or when we might need all we had. On account of this general extortion I remember, in particular, one Chinese shopkeeper who would not allow himself to be overpaid. Would I knew his name so that I might record it.

Besides food we tried to make other purchases. Shoes, socks, trousers, and shirts were in demand as were also tin mugs, spoons, forks, knives, and soap. Most efforts to buy clothes were unsuccessful; for any articles there were were made for the Malays or the Chinese, and as they are much smaller in build than the average Britisher the clothes, besides being of a different 'style', were much too small. Sid and I went on a shopping expedition and we each got a tin mug, plate, and a fork and spoon to assist with our eating. It was not possible to get into the shirts offered, but in order to use the soap we had bought on our shorts we each got a pair of Chinese trousers. Chinese trousers are to our eyes strange garments. These were, of course, not tailored in the West End, but like all Chinese trousers the legs finished half-way between the knee and the ankle and the garments had no pockets or buttons anywhere. Further, there was no difference at all between the back and the front and the joins in the cloth came in awkward places. They were kept in position by a piece of string tied above the bread-line, which in Sid's case at least was now less marked than formerly. Utility garments in very truth they were. We also bought—at great expense—two pillows, not the sort of pillows one gets in the Grand Hotels of the world, but comparable in length, width, and thickness to a folded pre-war newspaper.

It was at our first meal on Sinajang that I met one of the outstanding personalities of this mass evacuation. Sult Cunningham Brown was a well-built fellow of medium height with very fair hair and a winning smile. He had unlimited charm and a boundless energy. In the days that followed everybody knew Cunningham Brown, everybody brightened when he appeared. He seemed to be in his element in this kind of show and many owe much to his energies and cheerfulness. He always looked clean compared to us, he had always got a cigarette or a tit-bit of some sort for those he met; how he got them is a mystery. He used his great energy in going about these islands. Night or day, sea or land seemed the same to him; he took them all in his tireless stride. He found boats, collected people and transported them on stages of their journey, leaving them happier and more hopeful than he had found them.

We talked to Cunningham Brown during this meal. Characteristically he had produced some whisky and cigarettes for us because "you have just arrived from Pompong". We drank the whisky and water from a china bowl and smoked the cigarettes while we listened to his account of what had happened and what he hoped to do. He had secured a launch from somewhere but the engine was giving trouble; however, he hoped to search all the islands and collect everyone including those on Pompong. For the latter purpose he hoped to get Chinese tongkangs. When everyone had been got to some suitable centre he wished, he said, to get a few of the bolder spirits together and make a bid for Australia. I was anxious to join in this bid for freedom, but I suspected at the time and afterwards learned that such a route was as near as anything to impossible. Whether Cunningham Brown ever essayed it I do not know. He left Sinajang that evening, bound for Pompong and the intermediate islands, and although his launch broke down he accomplished the journey by oar and sail.

I spoke to little Jean Duncan about the same time. She was eleven years old, I should say. Her mother had been killed while embarking at Singapore and she had continued the journey in someone else's care. I was able to tell her that I had seen her father alive and well shortly before I left Singapore and this brought her a little comfort. D. H. Kleinman, well known in Singapore for many years as one of the best tennis players Malaya had ever had, was also there, badly wounded and lying on an improvised stretcher. I talked to 'Kliney', as we called him, and he was very depressed; referring to the many happy tennis functions we had had in days gone by he finished with, "and to think that it has all come to this". Poor 'Kliney' died shortly afterwards in Dabo Hospital. His name will long be remembered by many Malayans.

Dr. Kirkwood was also there when I arrived. He had brought a Red Cross launch from Singapore after the city had fallen and he informed us that the Japanese had always respected his flag. He sailed away with his launch that day, taking some wounded to Dabo, and there he did excellent work in the hospital among the victims of the bombings.

The women here were living mostly in the 'headquarters building' and the men were scattered in houses around. The seven of us who had come together from Pompong were given a vacant house nearby, and there we lived for the next few days, sleeping on the wooden floor at night and sitting round the door in pensive mood during most of the day. We had, of course, certain tasks to perform: we swept the 'headquarters building', and the path and drains in front; we swept our own house and tried to make things as clean as possible—a rather discouraging task. We washed our clothes, such as they were, one garment at a time, so that we should not go too short. We boiled water and helped Mrs. Moncur, who acted as head cook in her job of preparing the meals for all.

Every morning there was a sick parade and nearly everyone was in it. Medical supplies were short, but there were still some left, and there were women doctors and sisters in the community. Wounds, cuts, and bruises were getting troublesome; they would not heal on account of the poor condition of the patients, so many were going septic and very nasty some of them looked. The doctors and sisters here, as elsewhere, did valuable work and deserved our gratitude and praise.

I cannot say that we enjoyed being at Sinajang, but in retrospect it stands out as the pleasantest place we encountered on our flight to safety. Here we had a fair amount of food with a little variety, a roof over our heads, water to wash with, and a small party of congenial people for company. The big worry was how we were to get away; the lack of transport was serious, and we were fighting against time. Sid thought that we had already lost that race, and the sanest thing to do would be to go back to Singapore and give ourselves up. It would, undoubtedly, be better to be caught in Singapore than on these islands, as there, at least, we would be among our associates and we would have a better chance of getting proper treatment as prisoners. This was logical enough, but while there was a chance of escape

I preferred to keep on hoping, and in any case I didn't see how we could possibly get back. If there was a boat to take us back it could equally take us on.

This opinion obtained for Sid an opportunity of going off on the first boat which came along. Some gunners who had been stationed at the Changi end of Singapore had escaped in a small launch and they arrived with it at Sinajang. They offered to take as many as they could to Dabo, on Singkep island, where another colony of refugees had started up. It had been decided that this was the next place to go to as it was a larger village, had more accommodation and was equipped with a hospital. From information received by the Amir, the food position was not much better, if any, on Dabo than it was on Sinajang, but as a bigger place it had better prospects both of getting supplies and of contacting transport. Salmond held a meeting with a few of us to decide who should go off on this boat. The sick and wounded were the first on the list and then the nervous and depressed. Some thought that Sid was depressed and suggested that he might go, but he denied depression and, as I was not offered a place, he would not go without me. Mr. Samuels was then offered the place, and it was typical of the state of nervousness and uncertainty in which we all were that he took a great deal of persuading. He thought that the Japanese might already be in possession of Dabo and he had ideas of remaining on Sinajang and 'going native' till the end of the war. In fact, after agreeing to go, he changed his mind and the place was ultimately given to someone else. The boat set off in the afternoon and the gunner lads delivered their load safely to Dabo.

Those of us who were left continued to sample the 'delights' of the island. The day usually started for our party when Robertson went to the coffee-shop and brought back cups of coffee for us all, after which some of us would go to the other side of the island and bathe off the sandy beach. We would do the cleaning and brushing and finish by washing ourselves and perhaps some of our clothes. We did not wear much clothing for, as Sturt aptly remarked, there was no good sweating into a shirt when you had to wash it yourself. At 10 a.m. we had our morning meal, and shortly after we were almost certain to have an alert as the reconnaissance planes came over. The early afternoon was reserved for a siesta, and the evening meal was at 5 p.m. Sid and I usually went for a walk before dark and, as ever, with an eye to the future, Sid made extensive enquiries as to the sources and quantity of food available to the island in case we had to make a prolonged stay. The result was not encouraging; everyone said that formerly they used to get this and that, but now they didn't get it. It is a particularly hopeless task to argue with a Malay that this or that might be done when he has a rooted conviction that the fates are against him, or to suggest to him a new way of accomplishing something which he and his have accomplished in their own way for generations. Things were *banya susa* ("very difficult"), and that was that.

Darkness fell about seven o'clock, and at that hour we retired to our allotted places on the floor of our hut. Here we were troubled, as often after, by snoring. It irritated Sid in particular, and he often took drastic action to stop it in his immediate vicinity. I sympathized with him, for I failed to see why anyone should suffer from this distressing complaint, when with a little practice and a little will-power anyone can keep a shut mouth in sleep. The floor we slept on was more level than our jungle bed on Pompong, but not much, and it was far harder. Our bones which, from lack of abundant food, were nearer to the surface than formerly,

116

suffered much from their inferiority to wood. They seemed to be all over our body and in all the wrong places. Flat on one's back seemed to be the best position to start off with, but after the first awakening there was no best position, not even a better position.

Reckoned in days and hours we were not long on any of these islands, but to us the periods seemed to resemble eternity. The anxiety caused by the desire to get away quickly made time seem very long, and in spite of the tasks we made for ourselves much of that time had to be spent in sitting around smoking. It was here that we first learned to smoke the native tobacco rolled in a nipa palm-leaf. It was not a very satisfying smoke except for those to whom any smoke was good. Our 'landlord' would sit with us much of the time either to see that we behaved ourselves or else to get the crumbs which fell from the destitutes' table, for he always insisted on tasting any food we managed to get. He was continually asking us when we were going, which didn't help any as it made us feel more than ever that we were unwelcome—as indeed we were.

There was an alternative to the all-sea route to Dabo. One could do two short sea crossings between islands and walk across the islands from side to side. The walks were lengthy and difficult, and no one relished the idea of trying them in our ill-fed and bruised condition; but, nevertheless, we were making up our minds to the effort when we were saved from it by the return on Sunday, February 22nd, of the gunners from Changi with their launch.

This time they were able to take off all but a few, who got away a day later on another boat. So, as the films have it, we said good-bye to our colourful and picturesque island; but it was without regret on either side that the main street of Sinajang saw us no more.

117

CHAPTER TEN

SINGKEP

AS WE SET OFF on that sunny Sunday morning my thoughts went back to the many Sunday mornings in the happy days of peace when, in a similar launch, I would start from Singapore with a party of friends in the search of pleasure. On those occasions the launch was well stocked with good things to eat and drink and the passengers were in the best of good form, their only care in the world being to find a pleasant sandy beach somewhere on the islands immediately south of Singapore where they could bathe and laze the day away till the sun got low in the heavens. How different it was now; this launch was packed very tightly with people, dirty, ill-clad, and full of apprehension; they almost crouched in the bottom of the boat, and said very little.

There was certainly cause for misgivings. I was not, and I don't think the others were, very happy about this daylight trip, but the owners of the launch had insisted on it as they did not want to waste time. I spoke to Corporal Clarkson who was in charge of the crew and to his right-hand man 'Johnnie', but they seemed to think that the danger of attack was small so long as the passengers got under cover if planes came over; they themselves, they said, looked so like Malays on account of their deeply tanned skin and scanty ragged clothing that from the air they could not be identified. Nevertheless they kept a sharp look-out and handled the boat with a skill which did great credit to them, landlubbers that they were.

That the danger was not entirely from the air was soon impressed upon us, for Sinajang was still well in view when we spotted a launch somewhat larger than our own coming towards us. It was crowded with figures which looked more and more sinister as we got nearer. They were apparently soldiers wearing dark green uniforms, finished with military caps of what I choose to call the axis type. The craft and its complement resembled exactly what we imagined a Japanese patrol-boat would be like. Was this to be the end of our attempt to escape? Would this launch mean the beginning of our captivity? It looked very like it. We stopped our engine and waited for what was to come. The other launch also stopped its engine and we drifted cautiously together. The soldiers were armed, but they did not level their weapons at us and this looked hopeful, but still it was a very anxious moment. Suddenly a shout went up from one of our crew: "Hullo, Bob," and then there were relieved greetings from both sides.

The launch was manned by another party of soldiers who had escaped from Singapore possibly with little clothes. They had landed at an abandoned Dutch station on one of the islands and found some stores and the Dutch uniforms they were now wearing. They did not know where they were or what they were going to do. There seemed to be no one in command and altogether they appeared to be a somewhat irresponsible crowd. They had taken our launch for a hostile one, just as we had assumed that they were the enemy, and in consequence they were just as relieved as we were. We gave them some oil, which they needed for the engine, and suggested that they follow us, remaining about a mile behind, for we did not want to make ourselves more conspicuous or more suspected by the presence of two boats instead of one. They followed us throughout the day, but they added to our anxiety by continually keeping closer than we liked to have them.

The day passed without incident, but it was very trying sitting on hard seats in an open boat heated almost beyond endurance by a smelly engine and the blazing sun. Everybody looked completely worn out and dejected until in the late afternoon we had tea. It's wonderful what a cup of tea will do. One of the crew had spent most of the day in trying to boil a kerosene tin full of water on a delicate oil stove. Whether or not he succeeded I cannot say, but as the sun was sinking he decided that the moment had come. Somewhere in its wanderings the launch had picked up tea, sugar, tinned milk, and biscuits, and Clarkson's men were nothing if not generous. They fed some thirty of us with food and drink, which they might justifiably have considered was necessary for their own consumption in the days ahead, for well they knew that such valuable assets could not be replaced.

The tea worked wonders. It was the first that many of us had had since some time before Singapore fell, and for quite an hour our boat took on new life and cheerfulness. The sun, however, had almost completed its twelve-hour day in our service, and as the tropics do not boast a twilight worth mentioning it was obvious that we were not going to reach Dabo on Singkep Island before the light was gone. It was too dangerous to proceed in the dark, as the waters here were spotted with rocks as a Dalmatian is speckled with spots.

Unlike our other island homes Singkep is a large place and we had, for the previous two hours, been travelling along its coast line. Now we saw a few huts on the beach and, dodging the rocks, ran for the shore and grounded on the sand. Here we must stay for the night. We disembarked and, needless to say, were not plagued like most travellers with customs and emigration authorities; instead, who should be there to meet us, none other than the Colossus of the Isles, Cunningham Brown, bent on another rounding-up trip in the Sinajang district.

This night we built a cheerful bonfire in an open shed and had some more tea and biscuits, and what must have been positively the last tin of bully beef in the Malay Archipelago. The boatload of soldiers had followed us ashore, and how we all found accommodation in the few huts available I don't quite know. It was too dark to see, which may have been just as well. By this time a floor and a roof were all we asked, and I believe most of us got that.

By 11 o'clock next morning we had reached Dabo. Dabo had a pier of imposing length, but its main claim to fame and the real reason for the pier was the rich tin-mine which existed close to the village. The tin company and the Dutch Government had abandoned the site, the latter leaving one official, the Controlleur, to look after the place till the Japanese came to claim it. It had already been bombed and considerable damage had been done and, true to form, the enemy were sending reconnaissance planes over every day.

Here, for the first time, the Service personnel and the civilians were definitely separated. The latter, apart from the few sisters and nurses who went to the hospital, were accommodated in the fine residence of the Administrator of the tin mine which stood on a hill a little distance out of the village. It was indeed a fine residence, but the owner had packed up and gone, and though he had left much of his costly furnishings they did not afford great comfort when divided among the sixty-odd people now finding shelter there. Most of us slept with a thin mat or carpet between us and the tiled floor. It was the bungalow type of dwelling and there was no upstairs.

This was the main centre to which all the shipwrecked people had been gathered and many had come and gone before we arrived. Among those who were still there were several I had not seen before. These were survivors from the *Grasshopper* and *Dragonfly,* who had originally got on to different islands some distance from Pompong. Here also were some of those who had been on Pompong with us but never touched Sinajang. They had left after us in the Chinese junks which had taken the last batch from the island on Friday, February 20th. On that day three junks and the motor trawler had called at Pompong, and while the trawler had taken the P.W.D. contingent and some civilians straight to Sumatra the junks had brought the rest to Dabo.

Mr. Smart, Manager of the Federated Malay States Railways, and his wife were there. He was, so to speak, in command at this camp, and his wife was doing a great job of work on the feeding of the multitude. Sir John Bagnall, Mr. J. B. Ross, Mr. E. J. Bennett, Mr. A. C. Potts, Mr. C. N. Joyce, and Mr. F. W. Brewer were also there and many others. Mr. Brewer, whom I had known well for nearly sixteen years, did not recognize me, so dismal and dirty a figure I cut.

When we first saw the handsome bungalow in which we were to stay we thought, now for a proper wash, shave, and clean up; but, alas for our hopes, there was no water. The water had formerly been pumped by an electric pump from a well down on the level, but the pump had given out because the bombs or the Dutch had destroyed the electric generators. Here and elsewhere the Dutch were carrying out the scorched earth policy very fully. Nature came to our aid and sent rain, rain in which we stood naked and washed ourselves, and rain which we collected off the roofs and drank. Sid, the expert in such matters, confirmed that it was perfectly safe.

Tiled floors felt harder than wood or jungle and our nocturnal unrest was here aggravated by a great volume of community snoring. I, for one, certainly slept badly at Dabo; but it had one virtue, I awoke very early. Here truly the early bird caught the worm, the worm in this case being the odd bit of bread, fried coconut bun or banana which could be bought in the village. Just after dawn each morning many of the able-bodied went to the village to find if there was anything to supplement the rations served out at the bungalow. Any food there was came in in the early morning and one had to get there shortly after daylight. Most of the shops in Dabo had closed doors, as the owners had fled to the jungle for safety from the bombing, but here and there a timid door was half open, and if you penetrated the murky depths of the interior something might be found. There was also the occasional hawker in the street who might have some edibles, the history of which you did not care to investigate. Still, the food at the bungalow, which consisted almost entirely of rice and spinach, was so dull that any change of diet was heartily welcomed. As usual everything was most expensive and the trader certainly took his pound of flesh.

It was here that Sid began to suffer badly from an old, nasty and painful complaint which did not add to his 'pleasure' on the trip; in fact, he suffered considerably from then on. Most of us felt that the last two weeks were beginning to tell seriously on our health and strength. Our wounds, cuts, and bruises were getting worse instead of better, and the queue at the hospital twice a day during visiting periods was always a long one. Dr. Kirkwood was still here, and he with a number of the evacuees were helping to staff the hospital. Supplies, however, were short and dressings had to do over and over again.

There was still a feeling of optimism abroad. People talked glibly not only of getting to Sumatra but of what they would do when they got home. Sid and I often wondered if it was just talk or if they really believed that it would all be as simple as they indicated. We certainly didn't think it would be easy and, as events proved, we were nearer the truth than the others. When I was having my bruises attended to at the hospital a local dresser said to me: "All your worries are over; it will be easy from now on after what you have been through." I am afraid I laughed bitterly and replied: "Oh Yep," for I didn't see any possibility of an easy journey. First we had to get to the mainland of Sumatra, then across that country to some west coast port, and finally, if we ever reached that coast, it was at least probable that there would be no ship to take us away. How could it be easy? Once more I cursed wishful thinking.

The first difficulty was, as always, transport. We didn't know when any boats would come, or if they would come, and without good boats any further progress was impossible. It would need to be a useful boat to take us across the open sea to Sumatra, and it was a journey which should, most emphatically, be made at night because, for all we knew, the Japanese would be constantly patrolling this highway between Singapore, now undoubtedly a base of operations, and Java the present scene of the main fighting. Things didn't look too good for our chances of getting across at any time, much less during daylight.

The Controlleur possessed a wireless receiving set and so we got some news. At this time there were apparently still hopes of holding Java. Somehow it got around that engineers were wanted in Java to help with the construction of defences, aerodromes, and other military requirements, and so the engineers in our party were marked as the first to be sent off. Those of us who were of that profession felt the irony of the situation. For the first time in our lives we had people asking for us, whereas most of our adult years we had spent in trying to create a market. For the first time in our lives we had no means of going where we were required. One afternoon some of the engineers, including Sid and myself, decided to have a shot at getting a generator going so as to pump water to the bungalow. The only water we had had so far, apart from rain, had been brought up in tanks, and it was a very inadequate supply. We went down to the power station and to the well where the pump was, but we had little success. On returning we found that two boats had arrived, one a hospital launch which was taking off some wounded and the other a small launch manned by some planters from Johore. The latter had offered to take about ten people, starting off that evening, and the ten had been made up with the engineers who had been at the bungalow at the time and some others. As we were not on the spot we could not be included. We kicked ourselves, for while working in the common interest we had missed places in the boat which we most desired in the world. It couldn't be helped; we had taken on this somewhat hopeless task because we always welcomed any kind of job, one felt so impotent, there was so little one could do to help others or even one's self.

The boat set off but returned in about two hours. It had encountered heavy weather, and the passengers and crew, deciding that it was asking for trouble to go on, had returned with the intention of setting out again the next day. When the next day arrived two or three—thinking that the journey in such a boat was too risky—elected to remain and hope for something more substantial. Sid and I were given the chance of filling the places thus left vacant, and so when the boat left we were in her, although it was not very pleasant getting our chance in that way.

The weather this day was good and the sea was calm, but we were not so sure that we wanted good weather. True, we couldn't have it both ways, but on a cloudy and wet day we would have been much less likely to be seen by aircraft. That we were seen is almost certain, for we had not been going for an hour when nine Japanese planes hove in sight making towards us. It is easy to imagine our anxiety. Would they or would they not? Only time would tell. There was nothing to do but keep on going and cover up anything that might betray us as white men. Whether the planes had more urgent work to do, whether they were deceived or whether they were merciful, we do not know, but they turned away and left us. Once again strained and anxious faces brightened up with hope, and even the launch's little motor seemed to hum a different note.

Until evening we skirted the coast of Singkep, reaching just before dark its most westerly point. Here we stopped to await darkness and to take some food. In normal conditions the consumption of a meal means little, and is not worth mentioning, but to us every meal was an event. Food was of paramount importance. This meal was a goodish one for, like the other launch we had travelled in to Dabo, it was comparatively well stocked, and the owners were most generous with their larder.

I wish I had taken the names of these lads—all young—

who manned this boat. One of them was called Parsons, I believe. They were the only people I met who were really anxious to get into the fight again. They were, as I have said, rubber planters, but since the outbreak of the war in the Far East they had been serving with the Johore Volunteer Forces. Escaping in this launch, they were unselfishly using it and their resources in an effort to save the shipwrecked people from the islands when they might easily have made an early bid for safety through Sumatra with every chance of success. They were doing the same job as Corporal Clarkson and his pals, and as Cunningham Brown was doing in his unique way. These men were the real heroes of this mass flight. They had, it's true, an opportunity which others hadn't on account of possessing launches, but, though not sailors, they used the opportunity in the best traditions of the sea.

As night fell we started off on the critical stage of our journey, the open sea stretch across to the mainland of Sumatra. "If we keep going north-west we are bound to get somewhere near the mouth of the Indragiri River," was the way the skipper summed up the navigation problem. He knew this from a study of a chart which had been on board earlier in the day. The chart had blown overboard, but it did not seem to worry the crew, they were full of confidence. At the same time it was not sufficient to get 'somewhere near the mouth of the Indragiri River'; it was very desirable that we should get exactly to the mouth of that river for two reasons. If all went well we were going to hit the other side just about dawn, and the sooner we got into the river the greater was the chance of our not being discovered. Again, if we struck coast north or south of the river mouth we would have no means of telling which, and we might tum in the wrong direction along the coast and, apart from not finding the estuary, would very likely run into trouble.

There was a compass on board, but the only means of seeing this was by putting a lighted candle in a pocket at the side. The candles burned very quickly in the wind, and the crew soon ran out of them. I produced the stump of one which I had picked up somewhere, but that soon exhausted itself, too. We then had to fall back on lighting a match every now and then to see if our course was approximately correct. After the first few hours the moon and the stars appeared from behind clouds, and most of our steering from then on was by the light they gave. I spent most of the night in the stern giving a hand with the navigation, about which I knew a little. I was in an anxious frame of mind when the night began, and had tried unsuccessfully to sleep a little farther forward in the boat. After we had been going for about three hours in the darkness I noticed a smell of burning. It got stronger and stronger, so I got up to investigate, and found some boards round the exhaust pipe on fire. Without stopping the engine or showing any particular concern the crew put out the fire, but I am afraid it shook most of the passengers; a fire on top of their other worries was not at all to their liking. From then on I stayed with the helmsman, too roused to attempt sleep.

There is something enchanting and unearthly about being in a small boat far from land when the moon and stars are shining overhead as they do in the tropics, and this night as we pushed through the choppy water I found it very difficult to comprehend that my situation had anything to do with reality. It felt more like a dream than anything I had ever known. For hours no one spoke, there was no noise save the spluttering of the engine and the splashing of the waves. We seemed to be journeying through time and space with no yesterday and no tomorrow. The past seemed so unreal as to be untrue, and the future was too uncertain to be real. With the nose of the little craft pointed at a star I hung on to the rudder, trying to keep my grasp on this earth by the feel of its roughened surface.

When the night was well advanced the choppy sea turned truculent, and our boat heaved and tossed so that everyone was thoroughly aroused and the necessity of keeping one's balance and keeping very chased away all dreamy feelings and all unearthly thoughts. When the heaving and tossing had continued for some considerable time and we had had about enough of it, the ragged waves eased down and changed to a smooth swell. In case we should become too happy at this relief, Fate decided that we must have another little upset to balance things. Our engine stopped. "Put some more petrol in," said the skipper, and in more petrol went. But the engine was having none of it, at least not immediately. After a day and night of hard work for a very little engine a rest was due to it—and a rest it had for the next twenty minutes while as many of us as space would allow gathered round and touched this and that, here and there, during which time the remaining passengers thought up all the worst possible consequences of the engine's failure.

Illogically and unreasonably, but mercifully, the engine started up again after this protest, and seemed as lively and efficient as ever. Everyone felt relieved, but all was not over yet. Troubles never come singly, we had been taught; we had had a fire and an engine stoppage, what would happen next? Perhaps next time we would sink and sharks would finish us off. 'Why have ye so little faith?' The first light of morning came and though Jesus did not stand upon the shore, or at least we couldn't see Him, the shore itself was there—not a quarter of a mile away. The shore of Sumatra. Would I knew what everyone's thoughts had been during that long night. What fears, hopes, loves, passed through each man's mind. One thing I am fairly certain about is that the sight of the coast raised our hopes inordinately, and we felt that now at last we had got our feet on to the bottom rung of the ladder of liberty.

For the moment no river mouth could be seen or anything to indicate in what direction it lay. It looked as if the best thing to do was to toss for it; should we go north or south? We did not toss, possibly because we felt it would be too flippant in the circumstances. Some of us looked wise and said, "It should be to the north"; the skipper tried to look as if he knew all the time, and so we turned north. For hundreds of miles one part of the coast looks exactly like another in these regions, unendingly flat with trees right down to the sea, but by instinct or chance we had chosen the right direction, and we came to the river mouth, or, rather, one of its mouths, after going for about a mile. On the whole it had been a very good night's work; a handful of rubber planters had taken us by night across the seas almost as unerringly as they would have guided us through the sameness of their vast plantations in Johore.

Up the river we went; there was still a long distance to go before we might reach the village where our boat proposed to leave us and go back for more people from Dabo. Now the current was against us, and progress was slow. There was no food left, and the sun came out in all its fierceness. It was unwise to travel by day when it could be avoided, but if we had travelled by night only the delay would have been too great. So on and on through the endless hours we forced our way up the river, walled on either side by the thick unfriendly jungle. Malaya and the East Indies usually surprise by their greenness and freshness the visitor who comes for the first time. The visitor has heard of the boiling sun and has seen on the map that these lands cluster round the equator and, to the untravelled, these things mean burnt-up lands, sand, rocks, and coconut trees. What is overlooked is the abundant rainfall which keeps everything eternally green, no leafless trees, no dead grass, no matter what time of the year you come. The jungle is usually thickest at the edge of an opening, and there is no seeing through it or over it, so that all one sees on a river like this are the green walls on either side. An unusual and fascinating sight at first, but to those who know it well it becomes, after a while, terrifically monotonous. We who were scorched by the sun, cramped and stiff from sitting on hard seats and in unusual postures, hungry from lack of food, apprehensive of danger, tired, weary and bruised, got no relief from looking at the jungle.

With us on this stage of the journey, if I remember aright, were Messrs. Joyce, Peakes, and Riviere of the Cable and Wireless Company; Mr. A. C. Potts, of the Commercial Union Insurance Company; and the architect, Mr. F. W. Brewer. Others I have, for the moment, forgotten. Names seemed to matter little just then, and the meeting and leaving of this or that person was of little account. If you met someone you had known before you were surprised to find him there or glad to see that he was alive and still in the running. Apart from very intimate friends, one man was the same as another—all refugees, all destitute, dirty, and about to lose hope, if, indeed, they had not lost it already.

132

Morning wore to afternoon, and all bad things come to an end just as surely as all good things, if not as quickly. About two p.m., after twenty-seven hours of discomfort, to put it mildly, we reached Tembilahan, a little village on the left bank of the Indragiri, some thirty miles from the mouth. Cautiously raising ourselves on stiff legs we set foot in Sumatra.

CHAPTER ELEVEN

INDRAGIRI RIVER

OUR FIRST ENCOUNTER WITH THE PROMISED LAND of Sumatra was anything but attractive. The wretched little village of Tembilahan had been made more wretched by the recent rains, which had filled all the pot-holes in the ill-made roads with water, and the ditches which skirted these roads were overflowing with foul slime. The dilapidated shops were mostly deserted, and the whole place looked abandoned and forgotten. We felt instinctively that this place was a bad omen for our journey across Sumatra; a successful journey could not possibly start at such a place.

We were desperately hungry, as we had not eaten since the night before, and we had hoped to get a good meal at this village. Alas for our hopes, we hit a bad snag right away. Up to the present we had been using Straits dollars for all our purchases, and naturally these were not used here. We had expected, however, to be able to change them into Dutch guilders, but we soon learned that the Netherlands Indies Government had closed down on accepting Straits currency since Malaya had fallen into the enemy's hands. We could, at first, purchase nothing.

Rumours had reached us in Dabo that a highly efficient

organization existed for assisting refugees across Sumatra. This was supposed to consist of a series of camps an easy day's journey apart, with transport facilities for taking large numbers of people from camp to camp. This was certainly the idea aimed at; but it was, through no fault of its own, far from efficient. I am unable to say what the true history of this organization is, but it seems certain that it was of military origin, and when first conceived it was intended to assist only a small number of Services personnel whom it was expected would make their escape from Malaya. In fact, a great many more than was expected did escape, and on top of this the organization had to deal with all the shipwrecked persons an addition which had never been contemplated. How far this organization was official I do not know. An Army officer in Tembilahan told me that he had been sent to Sumatra as early as February 2nd to get this thing going; but, on the other hand, officers at other camps impressed on us that the whole thing had just sprung up on account of the demand, and that they had no resources other than those being generously afforded by the N.E.I. Government. The organization was inadequate because of the unexpectedly high numbers and the late date at which many of these had arrived. Those in charge of the camps from time to time did all they could, and I believe that in the early days after Singapore had fallen the journey across was comparatively comfortable and speedy. With advancing time, however, the transport largely dried up, and the journey became anything but comfortable or speedy. Still, any refugee who arrived at Tembilahan, Rengat, Ayer Moleh, Toleuk, Sawah Loentur, or Padang, got a roof and a little food of sorts for nothing.

We did not know all this at the time. We had landed in Sumatra with high hopes of a quick, safe, and relatively comfortable trip to the west coast. Tembilahan damped our hopes but did not crush them, for we had noticed a good-looking if small steamer lying at the landing-place, and this might well be our transport for the first stage, as indeed it was, there being no road from Tembilahan to Rengat, the next camp.

The officer in charge got us a meal of sorts, thirty cents' worth of rice and ducks' eggs, at a miserable little coffee-shop in the village. He paid for this from the organization's funds, which, so far as I could gather, were acquired on the 'lease-lend' principle from the N.E.I. Government. About an hour later the same Government here extended its generosity to the extent of changing into guilders not more than five Straits dollars for each person. I must not create the impression that everyone had money. That was not the case by a long way. A great number had no money whatever, having lost everything when the ships went down, but some had been able to bring their wallets ashore with whatever happened to be in them, and those who were thus fortunate were sharing with the penniless.

When we landed we were shown to a small go-down or warehouse with a concrete floor and a tin roof which was to be our quarters while we remained in Tembilahan. It was a miserable place, and did not increase our desire to sojourn in Tembilahan any longer than possible. Fortunately we did not even have to spend the night here, for we set off in the small steamer that evening.

After getting our money changed we toured the village, hoping to pick up some fruit and any little thing such as a piece of soap or a comb, which might help to make our lives less miserable. We visited the local clinic to have our dressings changed; but, while they did what they could, they had no supplies, and could not even produce hot water. We talked to those in charge about getting on and were told that we might get away that evening, but it wasn't certain. This uncertainty made us depressed; then it rained, we got wet, and we became more depressed. In fact, my over-riding memory of Tembilahan is one of complete wretchedness. This wretchedness was relieved momentarily by meeting with Company-Sergeant-Major Flannigan. He stood outside our go down pouring forth a tirade of highly ornamental words at some soldiers who were doing something he didn't like. This C.S.M. was more like the traditional British soldier than anyone I had ever met. He had a marvellous vocabulary, an abundant sense of humour, and a heart of gold. He did what had to be done at the moment, and his actions were not weakened by the pale cast of thought. His rich Irish accent made me homesick.

It is illogical to argue from the particular to the general, but I feel very much inclined to say that the men who go down to the sea in ships have very little sense of time. I have travelled a good deal, and I have frequently been annoyed by the hopelessly bad estimates of time given me by officers of ships when they tell me how long it takes to get to a place by sea or river. This time I was told that we would reach Rengat the next morning early, and as a result of this misinformation Sid and I spent another twenty two hours without food.

We embarked on the steamer *Kingfisher* about 6.30 p.m. on Friday, February 27th. Captain Macdonald, a Scots Army officer, was in command of the steamer, which had originally, I believe, been worked between Singapore and the islands in the Rhio Straits. Before boarding her we said good-bye to the Johore planters, and wished them luck. They were setting out to retrace their course to Dabo to bring more people to Tembilahan. We never saw them again, and we heard later that the Japanese had occupied Dabo before they could have got back. I sincerely hope that they didn't run into the enemy. They had deserved a better fate than that.

When we embarked it looked as if there were to be only some ten civilians and a few soldiers on board, and we arranged ourselves on the deck with a certain amount of space and as much comfort as we could. Before we sailed, however, two more Darties arrived. One included Sir John Bagnall, Mr. Bennett, Major Scroble-Nicholson, and other civilians, and the second was a large party of soldiers. This meant a rearrangement and the available space was taxed to the limit. We were packed like crackers in a box, but not nearly so ornamental. The only accommodation was on the deck, which had a much-torn awning over it, and a hold up for'ard which had almost no ventilation.

As we got going it started to rain, and we tried to get our heads at least under the intact parts of the awning. As we were very sleepy this sufficed to let us get a few hours' uncomfortable slumber; but about midnight, I should say, the rain increased in intensity, and before long we were lying in pools of water and water was streaming down upon us. Getting up, I went down into the hold and found a few inches of vacant space on top of a barrel, where I sat, and putting my head against the side of the ship I dozed off again, to be awakened this time by a soldier who was having a bad nightmare. In his sleep he was again fighting the Japanese, and was about to make a counter-attack when I woke him in the interest of all in the immediate neighbourhood.

In the early hours of the morning the steamer stopped; the rain had become so heavy that it was impossible to see, and the Captain, fearing she might run aground, decided to stay put for the night. At dawn we got away again; but all day we had intermittent heavy showers, when we got more or less wet. On account of being told that we would arrive at Rengat in the early morning, Sid and I had brought no food, and all day we went hungry. It was a long day, unrelieved by any scenery except the green walls of jungle, or any incident which might help to break the monotony. We were glad of the latter, for all incidents in our lives in recent weeks had been of an undesirable kind. We still feared that aircraft would get us. A boat on a river would be easy prey, and this was the largest craft we had been on since the *Kuala*.

One memory of this voyage sticks in my mind. A lad, whom I will call the ship's cook because he cooked food for the crew, was continually singing. It probably impressed me because it was so long since I had beard anyone sing. He was just someone who had escaped from Singapore like ourselves, and not a ship's cook, but he obviously had a knowledge of the culinary art and was lending a hand on the *Kingfisher* in the same way as many landlubbers were helping on boats these days. His cheerful outlook, which was to me a miracle, was not able to perform the other miracle of feeding the multitude which would have been so acceptable, and we continued to go hungry.

About five p.m. we got to Rengat and disembarked at a promising-looking village. This place went further towards fulfilling its promise as regards food than anywhere we had yet struck, but—. I will tell about the 'but' later.

We were met by Major Campbell and guided to an empty go-down near the landing-place. Major Campbell was, in the meantime, in charge of this 'camp', and now he addressed us from on top of a packing-case. He told us that camps had been established between here and the coast, at

Ayer Moleh, Toleuk, Sawah Loentur and Padang, and that great numbers of people had passed through here on this route, getting to the coast by easy stages on lorries and cars. At Padang they were being taken off on destroyers and cruisers, and perhaps other boats. The journey would be easy, especially after we got to Ayer Moleh; it would have been all right from here but, unfortunately, for some reason, the transport by road from this camp to Ayer Moleh had been withdrawn and we would have to go that stage by river. It was, however, only about seven hours up the river, and after that we would get road transport which would take us speedily along the remaining stretches. This was the worst camp, he said; it was a bit rough here, but at Ayer Moleh the accommodation was good, and we would be able to get a proper wash and clean up. In the meantime he had arranged a meal for us which would be along in ten minutes, and we would get another meal before setting out next morning. We cheered him. Here, for the first time, was a clear statement on what was happening, and what we might expect, and it was good news. Hitherto our information always had to be dragged out of those who knew. One crept up to the men who were running the show and beseeched them to tell what they knew, and the lack of success which invariably attended these requests was annoying. It must be admitted that it was like trying to get blood out of a stone; they really didn't know anything much, but a clear statement on what they knew or even what they did not know would have helped a lot by dispelling our uncertainty and counteracting rumours. Anyway, now we had been told without asking what the position was, and what was going to happen to us, and the statement was made with so much confidence and directness that we had no doubt whatever that the speaker knew what he was talking about, we were immensely cheered. Alas, in this uncertain world even efficient and sympathetic people like Major Campbell can sometimes be wrong, and very wrong he proved to be. No doubt he believed exactly what he told us, and had adequate grounds for doing so, but factors outside his control and knowledge took a hand in affairs, and our journey across Sumatra did not at all resemble what he described it as likely to be.

The meal he had promised us turned up-but it was a poor meal: just rice, a little vegetable, and a liquid which may have been intended to be tea. Fortunately, we were able to supplement this food in the village with other eatables a little more appetizing, and, on the whole, we felt reasonably well fed by the time darkness fell and we went to 'bed'.

As the reader will remember, we had, by this time, sampled a variety of sleeping places. We had been frozen on the wet sand, and bruised and frightened in the jungle of Pompong; we had slept on wood floors in Sinajang and tiled floors in Dabo. We had sought rest in the bottom of open boats and been soaked through on the deck of the *Kingfisher;* and now, on this night, we were given an abandoned school-house to make our home. The school-house had a concrete floor on which had been spread some time previously a thin layer of hay. It had obviously been slept on and walked over many times. The surrounds of the school were swampy, and one had to pick one's way carefully between pools to arrive reasonably dry at the entrance.

I think that, of all the nights we spent in unaccustomed places, this was the most miserable, apart from the first night on Pompong. No sooner had we settled down than mosquitoes by the million invaded the room. They attacked us at both ends and on the flanks, and they dived at us from above with unabating fury. In no time we were stinging all over, and our condition can be imagined by those who know the irritation which even one mosquito bite can produce. I covered myself completely with my share of the blanket and with other rags which I possessed, leaving only my nose uncovered for breathing purposes. Hitherto the blanket had been used to lie on rather than under, but now it had nobler work to do. These coverings reduced the number of mosquito bites I received, but did not eliminate them entirely, and to the mosquito bites were now added bites from hoards of unmentionable vermin which inhabited the bay.

The blanket on top was probably better than the blanket underneath, but very soon it became unbearably hot, and I sweated from every pore. I was forced to get up. I wandered outside and found that many others had been evicted in the same way. We splashed amid the mud and the water around the school, trying to evade the outdoor mosquitoes by movement, and as we passed each other all we said was "Isn't it miserable?" or "Isn't it bloody?" After half an hour of this I thought I would try to sleep again, for I was dead tired, and I went back to my former position on the floor.

I have never felt like murder, but if I ever had anything approaching lethal feelings it was that night. Two army officers in one corner of the room kept up a conversation in loud and penetrating voices, the sort of voices the Americans say that the English have when they hold conversations in railway carriages, filling the compartments with loud descriptions of their own ideas and feelings irrespective of who may hear, or of the discomfort they cause others who have no interest in hearing their thoughts prostituted before the world. The conversation, which no one could avoid hearing, much as they wished to, was fatuous in the extreme; it ranged over such subjects as advice on taking drink, how to go to sleep in spite of mosquitoes, the morals of Malaya, and other matters. The subjects chosen could scarcely have been more annoying. We had no drink, so the best way of taking it did not interest us, and only made us feel the deficiency more. The way to get to sleep was to forget all about the mosquitoes and say to yourself: 'I am going to sleep,' 'I am going to sleep,' over and over again. How to the devil could we forget about mosquitoes? Would they could forget about us. The opinions about Malaya got even further under my skin. In the room were many men who had spent all their adult life in Malaya, and here were two men expressing in a dogmatic way conclusions which they had come to in a few months, and which to us were completely erroneous.

A number of people gave up the attempt to sleep here. The mosquitoes, bugs, and bugbears were too much for them. They went outside and lay down on the pavements in the main street, and if they still suffered from the mosquitoes they at least escaped the other two pests. Later in the night I got a little sleep, but dawn was never more welcome.

We got a fair morning meal in the village, mostly of rice, as usual. Sid visited the hospital; his complaint was getting worse, and he was suffering a good deal. I was worried, for there was still a long way to go and obviously it was going to be very heavy going for him. Meantime, I went to the landing-place and found that many other people had arrived, in fact all who had been at Dabo with us. They had got a boat the day after we left, and had come straight through to Rengat. Cunningham Brown had also arrived from somewhere, bright and cheerful as usual. All who were now at Rengat were to proceed up the river in an hour

144

or so, bound for Ayer Moleh. It was thought that no more would now come from the islands.

Several boats were now at Rengat. There was the *Kingfisher*, which was marked for immobilization, as it was doubtful if she could go any farther up the river on account of the depth of water she would require. There was a hospital launch, a small naval patrol-boat and a shallow draught motor-barge known as the 'invasion barge'. There were also some barges without engine power and a Chinese tongkang. The 'invasion barge' was to take on the job of getting us all to Ayer Moleh. She was to load up herself and tow two other barges behind laden with people.

In the fast-running river the task of getting this convoy into shape was not an easy one. The 'invasion barge' was, of course, in front; behind her came a very large barge laden with men, and behind that another barge with women. The *Kingfisher* assisted in getting the latter two barges into position, and I spent a strenuous hour aboard her hauling on anchors and throwing ropes till my hands gave out. The second barge got into position, and was well secured to the first, but the third one gave difficulty and caused anxiety. She was got nicely into the middle of the river and the first two were to pass by close to her and throw her a rope with which she was to be made secure. The first time she failed to get the rope, so round we went and tried again; this time she got it, but on taking the strain it broke, so round we went another time. Going round like this was dangerous on account of the chances of getting on a mud bank and, of course, we were going down stream rapidly, the loose barge being without power. At the third attempt, however, she was made fast, and with a cheer we started up-stream.

A few were left behind to finish things off at the camp, and they were to come on by road in the only available car.

Cunningham Brown had attached himself to the naval patrol-boat and those on board her had some scheme of their own; what, I do not know. They stood on the starboard side of the boat waving us farewell, and I last saw Cunningham Brown as he was gaily kissing his hand to the last barge in our crocodile.

We had not gone far when our journey was interrupted by a stupid incident which frayed all tempers. One of the soldiers, doubtlessly very tired, had fallen asleep on the gunnel of our barge, and a lurch by the barge threw him overboard to wake in the muddy, swift-running water. Fortunately, he could swim, but he was quickly borne down-stream. The officer in command on the 'invasion barge', after an exclamation of anger, turned round in the river and the string of boats went down-stream to get behind him. It was a desperately risky procedure, but it was that or leave him. Well behind him we turned again, and got him when we were again facing up-stream. Naturally, the officer in charge was very angry, and he addressed us from in front. He said he was not going to risk the lives of forty women and others to pick up anyone else, so if anyone fell over he would be left. I think we all agreed with this, but the officer spoiled his case by adding on second thoughts that he would shoot anyone who fell overboard. This raised a storm of protest, and someone in the second barge who also had a gun replied: "You only need to miss once." In these days nerves were on the surface, and much of the primitive came out in many of us.

No one else fell overboard, but it would not have been surprising if someone had, for we were all packed very tight and it was necessary to sit in precarious places to get room at all. I was on the second barge, and beside me were Mr. Cairns and his little son of two years. How that child had survived so far was beyond me; only a superhuman effort by his father could have managed it. This day was immeasurably long and dreadfully hot. Slowly, ever so slowly, we made headway against the river; the journey seemed interminable. The boiling sun and, later in the afternoon, the tropical rain beat down upon us; many were scorched and all were drenched. Some there were who stood all day long, and there was virtually nothing to drink. Sid and I, mindful of the day before, had brought some food; but we had only the milk of a coconut to drink, which we shared with the Cairns.

How we hated this river, how we loathed the eternal jungle, how we would that day have given years of our lives to be clean and have an easy-chair to sit on. We tried to jest about coming here for a trip after the war, but the jests fell flat; we groaned and grunted and cursed our fate. The promised seven hours' journey took about nine, and by the time we arrived at Ayer Moleh we were completely worn out and sick at heart. From here on we had been told that everything would be grand; pray God that might be so. In that hope we stepped ashore and bade farewell to the Indragiri River. It had afforded us a route but, by all the devils, it had been hellish.

CHAPTER TWELVE

CENTRAL SUMATRA

BY THE TIME WE HAD DISEMBARKED at the rickety landing-stage daylight had gone, and we made our way to the camp in darkness. This time it was a rubber factory a few hundred yards from the river.

The women of the party were taken immediately to the local hospital two or three miles away and were accommodated in the quarters there. This was the last we saw of them or of any of the women and children who had left Singapore on the *Kuala* with us. The rubber factory, obviously an important place, had been abandoned just as it stood. The large corrugated iron buildings were full of machinery, washing tanks, rubber sheets, latex cups, and all the other tools and products of the trade. The buildings were scattered over a considerable area and the inmates of the camp were sleeping on the concrete floors of all of them.

Squadron-Leader Farwell was here and he explained to me the position. There were now over seven hundred people at the camp, fifty-nine of them civilians and the rest Army, Navy, and Air Force. Some days ago all the available transport had been withdrawn by the Dutch Government to move troops in Central Sumatra, as the Japanese were approaching from both the north and the south. Up till that

149

time the Government had provided buses and lorries to take the evacuees to the next camp at Toleuk, eighty miles away, but now it looked as if there was no means of going farther. That was the news we had to sleep on.

One of the officers who was helping to run the camp took us *en masse* from one building to another to look for some space where we might shake-down. He failed to find any, and finished by letting us hunt among the recumbent bodies ourselves for a few square feet here and there which might be used as a sleeping place. Sid and I found, near the door of one of the buildings, a place just about big enough to allow us to lie down. It was filthy dirty, but there was nowhere else. Every square inch seemed to be occupied, and we could only move about the building by taking the greatest care not to tramp on anyone's toes, either literally or figuratively.

Next to us we had some unexpected companions. Six Japanese prisoners-airmen, I believe, who had been brought all the way from Singapore with an armed escort. They were extremely muscular and well-built men and looked in the best of health. They sat round in a group and played cards during the whole of the time we saw them, and they looked far from depressed. I was told that these prisoners had left Singapore on the *Grasshopper* and, after the bombing, helped all they could with the survivors and proved useful on the island on which they had been cast up. Still, they were not the companions I would have chosen to sleep beside in a lonely factory in the heart of Sumatra under the conditions prevailing.

We had no sooner settled down than planes were heard over head and most of us dispersed into the rubber plantations, to return later in a wetter and dirtier condition than before. The mosquitoes were also bad here, and the concrete floor was hard; but I, for one, was so exhausted that I fell asleep almost immediately, and only woke with daylight.

The food position was exceedingly bad. The two meals a day which we received consisted of sloppier and more repulsive messes of rice than anything we had hitherto seen, and it was not flavoured with anything one could notice. The rice was eaten in most cases from latex cups which the soldiers and others had picked up around the buildings; although very uninviting-looking vessels I do not know what we would have done without them. The water, as usual, had to be boiled before drinking, and did not look too good even then, but there was plenty of water for washing in, and by using the tanks we managed to get our bodies clean. This was a great improvement.

The native village of Ayer Molen nearby boasted a local Chinese barber, so Sid and I decided to have a shave and thus he lost his shapely ginger growth and I said good-bye to my very unbeautiful brown and grey one. With the wash and shave our morale in creased, and this may be partly responsible for our impatience to be on the road and our determination to do everything to hasten our journey and, if humanly possible, to elude, even at this late hour, the rapidly approaching enemy.

Early in the day we had been told by the Colonel in charge at this camp that he had failed in all his efforts to get transport to take us on. It was not a question of money or of petrol, but there were no vehicles to be had, the Government had taken them all, and he did not know when any were likely to be available. In the circumstances he proposed to send us all up the river to Toleuk in two lots; the first lot of four hundred, all Services, would go that afternoon, and the second lot of three hundred the next morning. The civilians would go with the second lot, and the women, I gathered, would have to wait in the hope that road transport would come. The journey up-stream was likely to take forty-eight hours, and it was only possible because the rains had raised the river and made it navigable. The rains had also made the river flow faster, and it was impossible to tell if the launch which was now at Ayer Moleh and the other launch which it was proposed to get from Rengat would be able to tow barges laden with four hundred and three hundred people respectively.

It was a grim prospect. Even if the launches could do the job and with more rain likely it seemed to many of us an impossibility it was going to be a nightmare. Forty-eight hours in an open boat on that river on top of all we had gone through was something we had little stomach for. Crowded together we would not be able to move, and there would be no stopping-places. We would be scorched still further by the sun and drenched again night and day by the rain and probably, in the end, not arrive. We saw how wise it was not to suggest that the women should face it; it would certainly be beyond their endurance. Worst of all, however, to those of us who thought we could now go through anything, was the appalling slowness of this method of travel. Time was vital, we were cutting things very fine. To me, at any rate, forty-eight hours delay meant capture, and having got so far I was prepared to put everything into a bid to complete the escape.

Sid was one of the same mind, and we asked the Camp Commandant if he had any objection to us trying on our own to get on to Toleuk if needs be by walking or cycling or any other way. He had no objection, as he was not concerned with civilians, but warned us that if we got stuck up he might not be able to give us any assistance at a later date once we left his care. This did not seem to us to be of much consequence, as neither we nor anyone else had been travelling in the same party from the beginning. All had been moving as and when opportunity occurred, first with one party, now with another; and, certainly at this stage, speed was of much more importance than the safety afforded by numbers. In fact, the more people who had the courage and initiative to move on their own account, the easier it would be for the others; it would relieve both the food and the transport problems.

The choice before us was to wait for other people to act for us, to be one of a flock and probably get stuck in this desolate spot, or at best to face a long and useless journey up-river and get caught up in another perhaps equally desolate spot, or else to make a bold bid for it ourselves and thus make the task of feeding and transporting the rest of the party lighter. By this time there were no wounded or women with us; there was nothing we could possibly do to assist these seven hundred men except to improve their chances, albeit by an infinitesimal amount, by leaving them. As for ourselves, we were prepared to take the risk of running into danger alone, if by taking that risk we stood a chance at the sam time of getting quickly to the coast. It was rather like breaking out of a prison camp; those who were prepared to risk a graver fate might also eventually get to freedom sooner.

Besides his shirt, shorts and shoes, Sid's only possession not lost on the *Kuala* was a good wrist-watch. For some reason or other the Malays we had encountered on the way had admired this watch greatly. I had still some two hundred dollars which had, at this camp, been changed into a lesser number of guilders through the generosity of the

Dutch authorities, so with these assets we made our way down the village to see if we could do some bar gaining.

Our intention was to buy two bicycles, of which the village seemed to possess a number, so while the others were purchasing all the food they could find in preparation for the river route, we concentrated on bicycles. Every native we could find with a bicycle was approached and we offered the watch and money in exchange. We used all the persuasion we could, but though many looked longingly at the watch, none of them could be persuaded to part with a bicycle. Whether they thought there was some catch or whether our total wealth was insufficient I do not know, but part they would not. We then tried to hire, offering to leave the bicycle at Toleuk, where it could be recovered, but all was in vain. We had started out after two bicycles, but soon reduced our requirements to one, without any better success. During the afternoon we saw a bus, obviously on its way to Toleuk, laden with natives and all their household goods. These were running before the enemy also, and the sight of them did not console us in the least; it looked as if the Japanese were nearer than we had thought. We tried to bribe the driver to find a corner for us on the top of his already far overladen vehicle, but he also could not be moved. There was no room for us.

Footsore and weary we returned to the camp. It looked as if there was nothing for it, we must walk. On bicycles we thought we could do the distance of eighty miles in two days over the very rough roads, but by walking it would take us four days in our present condition, and this, while it would be surer and less un comfortable than by river, would not be any quicker. Still, we were determined that we should not go by river; and later that evening, before we left for Toleuk, we met others who were of the same mind and who were prepared to stay in Ayer Moleh almost indefinitely rather than face the river, but, of course, hoping that road transport would ultimately be available. Opinion against the river route was strengthened when it was learned that about fifty of the soldiers who set out that afternoon had been forced to return, as the launch could not tow them. This meant, in all probability, that three trips would be necessary, and the civilians, being the last on the list, would have to wait several days and then take the slow river route after that. This delay would almost certainly do away with any slight chance there was of getting through in time. For Sid and I the only question remaining was, should we start out that night or wait till early next morning? We were very tired, and it did not seem possible to start that night, so next morning it would have to be.

At dark, disappointed, tired, and disgusted with the camp meal we had just had, we decided to go to the village coffee-shop for a warm drink of coffee to ease our misery before turning in. In the shop we met Mr. Brewer and Mr. Potts, and we talked some time about our efforts to get on. They, too, realized that delay was fatal, and were desperately anxious to get away, but could think of no means of doing it any more than we could. After a bit they went away, and Sid and I had another cup to drown our sorrows.

Up to that moment we considered that in all our efforts to push the journey we had had no luck whatever. Every effort, every idea had met with frustration and failure. Progress had been slow, desperately slow, when the utmost speed had been called for. No one had seemed to listen to our repeated pleas for haste or, listening, had thought that it was impossible to do any thing more. Perhaps we were due for a change of luck; anyway, we got it.

To our table in the coffee-shop came a Malay and, sitting

down, he gave the usual greeting, *'Tabe, Tuan'*—(Good day, master); to which I replied, *'Apa kebar'*—(What news?), and so the conversation began. In the roundabout way so dear to the Malay heart we talked the local equivalent of cabbages and kings. We came at last to our story and our desire to get bicycles. Did he know anyone who would sell us a bicycle, we had money and a watch. No, he did not know anyone; bicycles were very dear. Yes, it was *'Banya susa'*; everything was *'susa'*. And then—you could have knocked us down with a *feather*—*'Kenapa tida pakai kreta, Tuan'*—(Why do you not use a car, master?) A car! Great green galloping giraffes! Had he got a car? *'Tida, Tuan'*—No, master). Then, why in the name of Mahomet had he mentioned a car? *'Sahaya ada kawan, Tuan'*—(I have a friend, master). The friend had a car and the car had some petrol, and he thought that the car and the petrol might be put at our disposal for the sum of—But what would we pay for it? Fifty guilders. Not enough; sixty guilders might do. All right, sixty guilders, and the bargain was struck. Sixty guilders, and we would have given all we had and almost all we hoped for to get that car. We didn't really believe it, and we were still more dubious when he said we would have to walk five kilometres out of the village to get it, and it could only take us to within seven kilometres of Toleuk. Nevertheless, any chance, however remote, had to be taken, and so we arranged with our Malay benefactor that we should go back to the camp and collect our belongings and meet him outside the village half-an-hour later.

Sid and I went back to the camp. We had agreed that we would take Brewer and Potts with us, if they would come. I had long before decided that the little money I had could best be employed, if opportunity occurred, in helping a few who had no money. Now the opportunity had come, and I was in a position to give three men who had no money whatever a chance to make a dash for freedom. Brewer and Potts, after a little hesitation, said they would throw in their lot with us. The latter said that if we ever got to a British port he could see us through financially from there on, and I might here say that he was as good as his word, and the first money we received in civilization was through him.

We told the camp Commandant that we were going and, laden with our miserable packs over our shoulders, we set off up the main street and out along the road to Toleuk. Our Malay friend met us as arranged and Sid, borrowing his bicycle, went on ahead to contact the car which was said to be waiting at a certain spot. Sid was raked with anxiety lest the car should not be there, and he pedalled for all he was worth, although it is probable that he had not ridden a bicycle for many years. He returned to us completely out of breath and overcome with excitement. The car was there all right and not so far out as we had expected and, cheered with this news, we pushed on, on weary feet, until the car appeared in the moonlight. It was near midnight.

Most journeys by passenger air services commence with a bus ride from some central point in a town to the aerodrome several miles out and likewise finish with a bus ride from aerodrome to town. In the early days of passenger flying I used to be greatly struck by the difference of tone between the first bus ride and the second. Passengers going to the plane were silent and anxious, in many cases it was probably to be a first flight, but at the destination, on the way from the plane to the terminal town, these passengers simple bubbled over with conversation. It was the relief of having passed through what they considered to be a dangerous adventure and the joy of being safe again.

That night inside our car a somewhat similar atmosphere

157

prevailed. We had all been almost in despair thinking that, after having escaped with our lives from bombs and sea and having made a long and miserable journey, we were going to be no better off than if we had stayed in Singapore. We were going to be captured by the enemy from whom we had fled and, in addition, we had gone through experiences of the worst kind. No wonder that we were cheerful as the car bumped along, taking us on another stage towards the coast at which we must arrive soon if we were to have any chance of remaining free.

It started to rain, and the rain came in through windows which could not be closed and seemed to blot out all visibility on the road, visibility already poor on account of the dimmed, war-time head-lights. We did not mind the wetting-much, but we feared dreadfully that the driver would run the car off the road and end our hopes. I am glad to say nothing like that happened, and we kept on going along the narrow earth and gravel road cut like a tunnel through the tall jungle. Twice we were stopped by soldiers at lonely outposts, but each time our driver jumped out and we saw something pass from hand to hand and we soon went on again. We asked no questions about the procedure and we were offered no explanation by the driver. We seemed to be getting along at a fair rate and that was all that mattered. Once at Toleuk we would be well on the way to the coast. We had been told that from Toleuk there was a bus service and also there were many cars, and transport would be easy. We had been promised, from time to time in the past, many comforting things and had been disappointed, so that now, as a rule, we believed nothing; but the news about the transport had come from a number of sources and we had hopes it might be true. After driving about three hours the driver suddenly announced that he would take us right into Toleuk, where we could put up at a Chinese restaurant. This was good news, as we had no desire to walk ten kilometres. Truly our luck had changed!

I wondered if it had. Twice before we had taken grave risks in the hope of speeding our journey and they were of no avail. We had left Pompong in a sampan rather than wait for a larger boat and, as a result, a number of those who had been with us there had already reached the coast some days ago and were on the sea bound for Colombo. This we had heard at Ayer Moleh. Again we had taken seats in a small launch leaving Dabo which others had feared to take, but all those who were with us at Dabo were also with us at Ayer Moleh, so that the risk added nothing to the speed of our journey. Now for the third time we had chosen to take the risky course in the hope of speed, and where it would land us I did not know. Perhaps the third time would be lucky; who could say?

In pouring rain we entered Toleuk about three in the morning, and our driver roused the old Chinese towkay, owner of the restaurant. He showed no resentment at being called out at this unearthly hour but quickly allotted rooms to us. Not so very long before we would have refused to test the pillows and mattresses we were now given to sleep on, but since we left Singapore we had not seen a bed or slept on anything above floor level, so it was not necessary to force us to get on these beds. Unused to beds I did not quickly go to sleep here, but instead lay awake listening to the rain which beat down with increasing fury. I had a feeling that this rain was not going to do us any good and, through the thin wooden partitions, I heard the others toss in bed restlessly, possibly due to the same thought.

Morning came and it was still raining. We wandered out of our rooms and noticed a Dutchman having breakfast at the far end of the passage. He greeted us in English, and we went and sat down with him. He told us he was a Police Officer from one of the islands and had arrived the previous evening bringing with him all the inhabitants of the village on his island. It was these we had seen pass through Ayer Moleh the day before on a bus. He was from now on to be Chief Police Officer at Toleuk. He ordered coffee and bread from the restaurant for us and produced from his room some eatables which we had almost forgotten existed: butter, jam, meat paste and, indispensable to Dutch breakfasts, cheese. It was the first civilized food we had had, and we felt we had indeed done a good day's work in coming to Toleuk. That food tasted good beyond description.

He got our story from us as we ate, and then asked us what we were going to do now. We told him we wanted to get a car to take us to Sawab Loentur and then on to Padang on the coast. "I will manage that for you," he said, and we were immediately on top of the wave. Here, indeed, was help. If the Chief Police Officer promised us a car then there could be no doubt that we would get it; arrival at Padang was assured.

There seemed to be no end to his generosity. He produced beer and biscuits, and then he said: "I see you are a little dirty, I will give you shirts," and straight away he went into his room and brought out four shirts, one for each of us, and good shirts they were. We protested, but we were very glad he would not listen to us. What a godsend a clean whole shirt would be.

The Controlleur sent for our friend and, buttoning a great rain coat about him, said: "I will see about your car in a little while." We tried to wash as best we could and, clad in the clean shirts, went down to the restaurant or Chinese eating-house, to give it a more appropriate name. It was damp and cold and the rain showed no signs of stopping. We sat about smoking cigarettes of native tobacco rolled by ourselves in flimsy paper. They were anemic looking cigarettes about as thick as a knitting-needle (number 6, ladies) and very untidy, but they had afforded us a lot of comfort from time to time. Brewer quickly had around him a crowd of natives from the streets as he recounted his adventures in Singapore and since. Brewer never tired of telling the tale to all and sundry whom he met, whether he had to tell it in English or in Malay bothered him not at all. Always a great talker, he had now a story of no little interest to tell, and he made the most of it to any handy audience. Where there is a show of any kind in Asia it never lacks an audience, and very soon the eating-house was full of dusky bodies standing about in awe or in admiration.

Sid and I were more concerned about the Police Officer's return and whether or not he would bring a car with him. We really believed he would; he had been so kind; he had even offered to pay for it. Surely he could not fail us. He returned all right, but would not talk about the car until we forced him to do so, and then slowly he admitted that he had not the power to get one for us. A car could only be got through the Controlleur, and he did not appear to wish to tackle that gentleman on our behalf. Not that we would have asked him had we known the circumstances in the first place, but he had said with so much confidence that he would get us a car that we had depended on it. Now this man who had given us so much could not fulfil his promise to give us the one thing we wanted above all others.

I faced the rain and went to the Controlleur's office. He was not very approachable nor had he a very pleasant manner in conversation. When I came to think of it, these things were understandable. He was undoubtedly a much-worried man; he had rendered all the assistance he could to many Britishers who had passed that way, but the demands were great. Much transport and food were wanted and he had very little of either; what there was of the first the Government wanted and his own people needed the second. Further, it must have been galling to him to see hundreds of Britishers using the resources of the country to make their escape while he had to remain and be captured. The Dutch did not try to evacuate their nationals from the Netherlands East Indies. They had no mother-country to go to; that had been taken from them by another enemy nearly two years previously and, further, they had made their homes in the N.E.I. to a much greater extent than the British had done in Malaya. There were far too many of them to contemplate evacuation; such a step would be impossible.

I asked the Controlleur if there was any chance of getting transport to Sawah Loentur, and the only answer I got was a shrug of the shoulders and a curt: "I have no car." As I was going, however, he said that there might be a bus still running and advised me to try that. This was good news and, having found out where to seek the bus, I returned to my companions.

A bus was, indeed, due to go the next morning at six o'clock, but we had to bribe the agent to sell us tickets. Though we chafed at the delay of another day it was comforting to know that further progress was possible, and we decided to possess our souls in patience.

Our Police Officer having now left the lodging-house we ate our tiffin of rice and our evening meal of the same cereal. Rice is like porridge in that it fills one up very full at the time, but departs quickly and leaves one very hungry.

No doubt it is possible to live almost indefinitely on rice and very little else. Boiled in water, strained and allowed to dry, it is very palatable when adequate spices and flavouring sauces are added, and one comes to like it more and more. We had had practically nothing else since Pompong, but we were always ready for more.

In the afternoon the rain ceased and we walked about the street and the path beside the river. We noticed with concern that the river was rising rapidly and, indeed, very soon the land on both sides of the main street was flooded. This looked bad for those behind us as it minimized their chances of making a successful trip by the river, and it also looked bad for us because our road onwards to Sawah Loentur ran parallel with and near to the river, and if that became flooded we could not proceed. There were a few soldiers and airmen here likewise waiting to be taken on, and they walked about buying and eating everything they could find. Among those I spoke to was one handsome fellow from an English village who was completely unconcerned and talked mostly about the beauty of the green foliage bordering the river. He wore nothing but shorts and shoes and his body was tanned a deep golden brown like the Balinese. This, combined with his athletic figure and fair curly hair, made his appearance very striking, and it was sad to think that, in all probability, he would soon be in a prison camp, and seemed to be quite unaware of the fact.

The bus which was to take us on to Sawah Loentur was scheduled to arrive from that place about six o'clock. As we sat in front of the eating-house talking to the owner we became increasingly anxious as the bus failed to make an appearance. One of the periods of anxious silence was broken by the towkay, who knew the difficulties we had had about transport and our fears for the future. *"Wang tida guna, Tuan* (money is no good, Master)," he said, which showed that the change in value of ordinary things had penetrated even to him. However, when on the next day he presented the bill, he was obviously of the opinion that it was still of use to him if not to us.

There was no sign of the bus before dark and it started to rain again. Hour followed hour and our ears got painful trying to detect the noise of a petrol engine. The agent told us, when we asked him, that it was likely to have been held up by floods. It was quite common, he said, and he would not know anything nor was there anything that could be done about it. Our appetite for rice left us, and we went to bed sick with another disappointment.

Through the night I woke at every unusual sound only to find that it was some variation in the intensity of the rain or of its direction. It came down in torrents and destroyed any flicker of hope we had. In the third Circle of Hell, Dante punishes Ciacco and others for gluttony by cold and heavy rain, but I felt with confidence that whatever sin I was being punished for by rain it was not gluttony. Someone must have pressed the wrong button, and pressed it hard, for the storm continued all night and into the next day.

Towards morning I did hear the sound of a motor and was getting up to investigate when Sid, who was even quicker, rushed out to see if it was our bus. He returned with the news that it was a lorry filled with people from Ayer Moleh. The lorry had turned up at that camp, and some soldiers and two of the oldest civilians had been sent here in it. The civilians were Mr. Samuels and Major Scroble-Nicholson.

After a morning meal we set out once again to see if any alternative to the bus could be found or if there was any other way of getting on. This did not seem likely with the road flooded, and we appeared to be stuck once again. We paid another visit to the Controlleur's office and he seemed to be in a more helpful mood than the day before. He pointed out to us on a map an alternative route to the coast via Pekan Bahru. It was a round about route, some five hundred kilometres long, and meant going back somewhat on our course, but it traversed higher ground away from the flooded river, and he thought that with luck we might get through that way. If we were prepared to try it and had money to pay for a car he would arrange the hire of one for us. It was a risk, we would be going nearer to the alleged Japanese positions, and if we failed to make it we would be stuck farther than ever from any possible help. Still, anything was better than delay, and we were out to take any risk provided there was a sporting chance of getting through.

The hire of the car was arranged and the four of us packed ourselves into it. We offered to take Mr. Samuels and Major Scroble-Nicholson, but the former did not want to chance it. Major Scroble-Nicholson elected to come and got into the car with us, but when we stopped for petrol at the end of the village he spied a soldier friend of his and went to talk to him. The friend persuaded him that it was a foolhardy attempt, and so he took his pack out of the car and bid us good-bye. He had no money and his presence might conceivably have made it more difficult for us, but so long as I had anything left I wanted to help anyone I could and I was sorry to see him leave us. I was, by then, convinced that it was this route or nothing, and I was right, for he was left in Sumatra.

We nearly met with disaster right at the start for, not half a mile from the village, we ran into a stretch of flooded road. Water came over the running-boards and our hearts were in our mouths, but we got through by the skin of our teeth and that was the last flooded road we saw.

We had started out about eleven o'clock in the morning and it was after 5 p.m. before we arrived at Pekan Bahru. On the way we crossed three ferries and traversed endless miles of indifferent road through the Sumatran jungle. We had rain and sunshine alternately but no incident—unless the purchase (at one of the ferries) of some of the best bananas we had ever tasted could be called an incident. The journey was a very trying one for Sid and Brewer; the former was suffering acutely from his old complaint, and Brewer was having trouble with a leg which had been injured in the last war. In cramped positions these two men were being hard put to it to stick the pain without stopping—and stop we dare not. Potts had cuts and bruises all over his body and an irritated skin, and I had septic cuts on my knees and feet, but neither of us suffered as did Sid and Brewer.

When we got to Pekan Bahm we went straight to the Controlleur's house and we found him in the garden, clad in trousers and a pyjama jacket. When he saw us he smiled, and that smile was full of sympathy, friendliness, and help. It was so long since we had seen a smile of just that calibre that we all started to talk at once. Sid drew himself up to the full height of his short figure and, putting his hands on his hips in characteristic posture, he announced that we were four shipwrecked mariners. Brewer started off in gushing words to tell his story from the beginning, and Potts started to tell his of the immediate past. The Controlleur had to stop them; he simply couldn't listen to everyone at once, and so I proceeded with an explanation of how we had come to see him in the hope that he would assist us to get to Padang. He told us he would help, but as we were obviously in a bad way we must first go down to the Government Rest House where food would be provided and a night's lodging furnished—all at Government expense. This sounded grand, but with an eye to the first necessity we pressed for information as to how we would get on next day. He said either a car could be arranged or we could go by the public bus. The car could take us to Padang in a day but it would be expensive, costing about forty-five guilders; on the other hand, the bus was cheap. The bus, however, would take two days and we would have to stay the night at a village about half-way. We had by this time just fifty guilders left and we agreed to take the bus on which, he said, he would make sure we would get seats. I don't know why we accepted the bus; it was contrary to all our previous decisions which had always been to push on by the fastest means irrespective of what it cost in risks, comfort, or money. I think with the proximity of the coast, the promise of a town where things to relieve our destitution could be bought, and the homeliness generated by the Controlleur's manner we were getting back the money sense; anyhow we agreed to the slow and cheap bus.

At the Rest House we were given a good tea, shown reasonably comfortable rooms, and promised a dinner at half-past six. It all seemed too good to be true; here was a paradise and to-morrow we would be on our way again. The tea must have brought me back to my senses, for I suddenly realized that we were being exceedingly foolish in choosing the slower means of transport, and I told the others that I was going back to the Controlleur to ask him to arrange a car for us even if it cost every penny I had got. As the money was mine they offered no opposition, even if they felt inclined to do so, which is doubtful.

I went back to the Controlleur and told him our decision,

and he readily accepted it. He called a car owner and asked him how much it would cost. The reply was sixty guilders and my heart sank, it was beyond our means. I had, however, reckoned without the Controlleur's generosity, for he immediately offered to pay twenty guilders towards it, and the car was ordered for 8 o'clock next morning. Not content with this he made me stay with him and discuss the situation over a bottle of beer and real cigarettes. He was, behind his smiling face and genial manner, terribly worried. His wife and child were at Fort-de-Koek, a health resort in the hills, while he had been ordered to stay on at Pekan Bahru to hand over to the Japanese. He was at present supervising the destruction of oil supplies, the small aerodrome nearby, and other things which might have been of value to the enemy. During our earlier conversation with him we had jumped out of our skins at a loud explosion and had not known what it was until he had explained that his men were destroying ammunition. He could not understand the rapid fall of Singapore, which he described as a beautiful place. The Dutch had always put their faith in Singapore while not neglecting their own defences. I left him in a pensive mood, and I can only hope that sometime I may be able to partly balance my account with him by rendering some service no matter what it entails.

Back at the Rest House I found my companions carousing with some Dutch soldiers over beer. These were the men who were scorching the earth before the invader. Grand fellows they were, and generous to a fault. They were indulging in an excess of jollity as men often will when the morrow holds for them an ugly fate. We all had dinner together and, for us, that dinner was a miracle, consisting of soup, meat, and potatoes—the first we had had of any of these—and finished off with a sweet and coffee. Our jolly companions left us immediately it was over and we were soon in bed.

Perhaps we deserved punishment for gluttony that night; anyhow, it rained as I have never known it to rain before. Many years' residence in the tropics had accustomed me to torrential rain, but that night it was more than torrential, it was indescribable in intensity. We had been told that there were two rivers to cross the next day, and if these were flooded the ferries would be unable to operate. If ever we should have slept soundly it was then, for relatively clean, well fed, well bedded, and very tired, we ought to have slept as we had not done for weeks. The rain spoilt it. Desperately anxious lest we should be denied our goal just when it was in sight we turned and tossed, listening to the incessant rain, hoping against hope that it would stop, but stop it would not. By morning I was in despair. I think that more nearly than at any other time on route I had given up hope. I probably exaggerated the danger of floods due to the weeks of anxiety and frustration I had experienced, but still the chance of being held up was very real.

The rain eased a bit about 8 a.m. and greatly to our relief the car turned up. We got ourselves into it hastily lest it should fade away and also because we wished to reach the ferries, which were at the near end of the journey, as soon as possible. The sooner we got to them the better was our chance that they would not have yet risen sufficiently to stop us and the sooner would our anxiety be over. In spite of our hurry, however, we felt we could not leave without dropping in on the Controlleur to thank him, as a party, for all he had done for us. The rain had somewhat damped even his spirits and, as he wished us good-bye and good luck, a wistful look came into ms eyes and his figure slouched a little.

With our hearts full of gratitude to the kindly Dutchman and feeling once again how unnecessary it was that these things need be, we started off on the last lap on land.

CHAPTER THIRTEEN

LAST LAP ON LAND

IT DID NOT TAKE LONG to get to the ferries and our fears faded away, for they were still working and the rivers were not particularly high, nor did it look as if the rain had been as heavy here as it was at Pekan Bahru. This was not surprising, for tropical rain is often very local, the beginning and finish of a storm being marked by a straight line across the road, one side dry, one wet.

These ferries were strange contraptions. They were constructed by placing a platform across three long open boats which acted as floats. The platform carried the car and passengers, and there might be perhaps a little hut built on it for the operators. They looked clumsy, and one wondered how they could ever be steered into position at the sides of the river and moved accurately across the fast-flowing current. The ferrymen, however, worked them with great ease and skill, if in a primitive way. They hauled the ferry upstream close to the near bank by means of a rope, just far enough up to allow the crossing to be made diagonally to the other side under the influence of the stream and two or three oars. They seemed to me the other side at exactly the right spot and were quickly tied in position with flimsy ropes to even more flimsy stakes, after which some bridging planks placed from ferry to shore allowed the car to be driven gingerly off.

With the ferries behind us we considered that there was nothing more to worry about until we got to Padang, so we tried to enjoy the trip as much as possible. As usual the scenery was almost exclusively jungle, but this time much of it was in mountainous country and some of the valleys and gorges were extremely beautiful. Unfortunately the rain started again and damped our pleasure, for we could see only short distances around. It might also have had other more serious results, especially if we had met a certain lorry first. We were climbing steeply up to high ground with perpendicular mountains on one side and a deep valley on the other. The narrow road was taking very sharp bends round the endless spurs of the mountains, and visibility was bad even on the short straight stretches. The conditions were just the sort to breed accidents, and an accident there was, but not to us. We came upon some Dutch soldiers standing in the drenching rain and they stepped out in front to stop us. They had been driving to Fort-de-Koek with a comrade who was very badly burnt when they met a lorry in head-on collision and both vehicles were crumpled up. They asked us to take the injured man on to Fort-de-Koek Military Hospital and we crammed him into the car. Like the great majority of Dutchmen from the N.E.I. he could speak English, and he told us that he had been burnt while destroying petrol. He had learnt, he said, not to destroy petrol in the regulation manner: next time he would use a method of his own. He was bandaged from head to foot and must have suffered agony, so with Sid and Brewer also in pain our car was more like an ambulance than anything else.

On we went to the top, then down again by means of nine

172

hair pin bends, one after the other, then along, then up again, and eventually we came to the very pleasant country near Fort-de-Koek. Here the sun came out, and the houses, as we approached the town, represented the first thing that we could reasonably call civilization which we had seen since leaving Singapore. It was a grand site for sore eyes and under any other circumstances we should have longed to tarry there, but now there was little in our minds but to speed to our destination.

We left the injured man at the hospital and thought once again what fine fellows these Dutch in the Indies were. He had said nothing about his suffering, though one could see that at times his pain was acute, and he spoke not at all about the future or what might happen to him.

Fort-de-Koek and the sun were left behind together, and as we made our way down to sea-level it was once again through drenching rain. About five o'clock in the afternoon the outskirts of Padang were seen and, very soon after, the town itself. We had learned that there was a British Vice-Consul at Padang who was handling the evacuation of Britishers arriving there, so we went immediately to his office.

Mr. Levison was sitting behind his desk looking tired and anxious, as well he might. He had for weeks past been consoling and assisting destitute men and women who arrived out of the Sumatran jungle. With little or no support from his Government he had been doing everything he could, cabling for ships, arranging money matters, billeting, making lists, and doing a thousand and one things which such a situation demanded. Knowing that hundreds had passed through his hands I spoke with an apologetic note: "I am sorry to say we are four more evacuees coming to look for guidance." "Sorry," he said.

"You ought to be very glad!" He then went on to tell us about some of the people who had been and gone and of the ships which had taken them away. He wasn't sure that any more ships would come, but there might be one or possibly two. He had just received a cable from Bombay, but he did not know what it was about, as the code was one to which he had not a key, so he had cabled asking them to send it in another code. It might be about ships, but again it might not. There was every chance that no more would arrive at Padang and, if one did, it might not get away again. The ships which had come previously had slipped in at night and gone off before daylight, for Japanese aircraft were over every morning and three ships had already been sunk in the harbour.

He then told us to go to the Town Hall, where billeting would be arranged, and he beseeched us to be courteous to our hosts whoever they might be because, he was sorry to say, that some others had not been. In the N.E.I. there is no colour bar to marriage or, for that matter, to many other things such as there is in most British colonies, and some of the evacuees when they had come up against this different order had not been very polite about it. Further, soldiers had sometimes got a bit rowdy and, to use his words, had "fornicated in public".

At the Town Hall we found the Burgomaster and others ready and anxious to help us. We were allotted billets and shown a dump of second-hand clothing from which we could select anything we wanted. Unfortunately, most of the normal-sized clothes had gone, and much of what remained had evidently been the property of very corpulent Dutchmen, of whom the Indies boasts not a few. From the Town Hall we went to the Club, at which a British colonel was administering to the needs of troops who arrived in Padang, and also arranging the order of evacuation when a ship came in. We registered our names and went off to seek our billets.

Sid and I were to stay with the family Van Der Hilst, and the others were each in a separate home.

Our hosts could not speak English so all our conversation was conducted in Malay. The Malay which the white man speaks is an expressive language, but is not usually capable of conveying fine shades of meaning in spite of this we got on very well and I think we made real friends of these generous people. Generous they were to a fault. Many kinds of food could no longer be obtained and all kinds were scarce, but they took all the titbits from their larder and forced us to eat them. Nothing that they had was too good to give us; they could not do enough for us; their sympathy and kindness were overwhelming.

That night, about 9 o'clock we had an air-raid warning, and all of us went into the little shelter in the garden. Planes came over head but no bombs were dropped; it served to remind us once again that the enemy were at hand when, with our improved circumstances, we might have felt inclined to forget. I noticed here that gongs were beaten all the time at the police stations during the period of the alert so that no one could be in doubt that a raid was in progress or enemy aircraft near.

For the first time we slept soundly and comfortably that night and awoke to a proper wash and breakfast. The morning was spent in buying some common accompaniments of life with our few remaining guilders. A cheap razor, toothbrushes, rubber shoes, and soap; such things as shaving-brushes, shaving-soap, and tooth paste were beyond our means. Our shopping was interrupted by the usual morning alert which, according to the residents, had occurred every morning for over a month at or about the same time. It was the usual Japanese reconnaissance plane come to see what was going on and if there were any ships in the harbour at Emmerhaven, the port of Padang. Later, when Sid and Brewer went to the hospital for attention, I helped Potts to bunt for a pair of shoes to fit him. Getting shoes to fit Potts was a difficult matter. He is a tall man with feet to match, and, after leaving Pompong, he had picked up a pair of canvas ones somewhere, but in order to get into them he was obliged to cut away the whole front part of the uppers, and like that they were not very comfortable, to put it mildly. Padang could supply nothing to ease the situation, so Potts' toes continued to stick out. Brewer, equally tall and weighing seventeen stone, had saved his shoes from the shipwreck, but the sole of one was detached from the upper part for half its length, and his condition was not much better. Nothing could be done in Padang to alleviate these foot troubles, so we went to the Club to see what effect a glass of beer would have.

In the Club we met a party consisting of six men who had been with us at Ayer Moleh. They were Sir John Bagnall, Messrs. Bennett, O'Grady, Cramer, McCardle, and Grant, who had got through from Ayer Moleh to Padang by using a car which they had been lucky enough to find and pushing straight on to Sawah Loentur the night that we had stopped at Toleuk, thus passing the danger spots before the river had risen and flooded the roads. Mr. J. Duke and Mr. Mackay were also there, but they had come sooner. Including our party of four there were now twelve civilians in Padang and, in addition, there were some Services men who had also arrived earlier. Others of the Services arrived from Sawah Loentur by rail in the afternoon.

After tiffin we made up further for loss of sleep by taking

A Chinese Tongkang

Moonlight in the Tropics

Malays

A Village in Sumatra

A Road in Sumatra

A Rubber Plantation

View from the Sumatran Hills

a siesta, following which our hosts gave us a cup of tea. It was almost like old times. I decided later to go by myself to see the Vice-Consul, as Sid, being in considerable pain, did not feel like walking. Mr. Levison asked me if I had been to the Club that afternoon for, he said, there was a ship in the harbour which hoped to sail at night. It wasn't a very big ship, he added, but I had better go and see the Colonel, who was arranging the list of people to go on her. Before leaving him I asked if he had sent out a copy of his lists of the people who had already passed through Padang because, I explained, friends and relatives would otherwise never know who had been lost at sea between Padang and Colombo or Australia or wherever else the ships had tried to reach. If I, for example, took the list away and got through with it then it would be known who had left Padang, and if they did not turn up at an allied or neutral port they could be presumed lost or recaptured, almost certainly lost on these seas. It would, at any rate, prevent much uncertainty. He admitted that he should have done that, but he had entirely overlooked it. He had only one copy of the lengthy list, and no assistance to make another, but, if I would come the following morning to help him, he would prepare a duplicate and try to get it off on any ship that might turn up. I promised that I would if I was still in Padang but, as things turned out, I had left by then.

When I got to the Club the Colonel said that if we came along at 9 o'clock that night we could go on a ship which was leaving before dawn. The ship was a small one; but it might be the last. I said: "We'll be there," although I felt far from sure that we would.

Padang must have been, at all times, a pleasant place, and that afternoon, bathed in sunshine, it was at its best. During the day we had had our clothes washed, and were cleaner and better fed than we had been since leaving Singapore. It would have been very pleasant to feel that this, our first taste of civilization for weeks, was the end of the journey instead of only a pleasant interlude in it. Indeed, I think some such feeling did creep into our thoughts. We were exhausted with trials and anxiety and were reluctant to admit to ourselves that perhaps the most hazardous part of the whole flight was still before us. Those who arrived at Padang soon after Singapore fell were reasonably sure of getting through to safety on any kind of ship, and some who had arrived later had been taken off on a cruiser. In our case the prospects were very different. Java had almost gone; the enemy's activities had penetrated far into the Indian Ocean, on and under the surface of the sea and in the air. There was no warship to take us away; the ship we were going on was a small freighter, undoubtedly slow. How nice it would have been to stay in Padang—Padang which looked so normal, Padang where we had been cleaned and fed. No wonder the poison of 'tidapa', as they say in Malay, or *laisser-faire,* as the French have it, came near to taking possession of our minds.

I went along to Potts first and then to Brewer and told them we were to leave that night. I did not put it as optional, for I wanted the party to commit itself before it had time to think: too much about it. I desperately wanted to go, for I realized to wait was folly, but I was frightened. I did not say anything about the kind of ship until it was dragged from me, and the news caused my friends' faces to fall, though in the presence of each other we refrained from expressing our worst fears. Not so Sid, who was always more candid about his feelings than the rest of us. He openly dreaded the prospect of going on a small, unarmed, slow ship across an ocean infested with the enemy. If anything happened there would be no handy island this time, and any lifeboats would almost certainly be destroyed when such a small craft was hit. "If I was not suffering so much from this bloody complaint," he said, "I don't think I would go."

"I think we had better go; we may not get another chance, and it would be silly to throw everything away at this stage. We must take big chances if we are to get away with it," I replied.

"If I don't go, will you go?" he asked.

"Yes," I said, trying to keep out of my voice any trace of faltering; but I felt then, as I feel now, that if Sid had stayed, I would have been with him.

My 'yes', however, seemed to settle the matter, and although we both dreaded the journey we did not again mention the possibility of staying.

Back at the house we told our hosts that we were off that night. It must have been done quite unconsciously, but they immediately related to us details of the sinking of ships near Padang, of the Japanese aerial watch over shipping and of the lack of speed of the type of ship we were to sail in. It added nothing to our peace of mind, and a close observer must have seen us wince from time to time. Fortunately, sitting in the growing darkness, our hosts could not see our faces nor could we see each other's.

The best that the house could produce was brought out for our last meal. In fact, I feel at a loss to describe the kindness and generosity of these people. They kept on offering us things from their household goods which they thought might be useful to us on the journey. It was positively embarrassing. We, however, were in no mood for considering our comfort; and worldly possessions, at that moment, meant nothing to us.

We four—and all the civilians I have mentioned as being

in Padang, together with thirty-eight Services officers and men—turned up at the Club at 9 p.m. as we had been asked to do. We sat down waiting for further instructions. After waiting a long time we lay down on the floor and some fell asleep. It was a long and anxious wait, but before midnight the Colonel came and said we must go to the railway station where we would find a train leaving at 3.30 a.m. which would take us the seven miles or so to Emmerhaven and the ship. None of us knew the way to the station, but the Colonel would not tell us; he said we had to find that out for ourselves. I have never been able to understand why he was so obdurate about this; he may have wished to avoid the accusation, however false, of giving wrong or insufficient directions. On the other hand, the station was not easy to find and the chances of asking anyone at midnight in black-out conditions were small. The result was that parties went off all over the place waking the inhabitants up to ask the way and shouting to each other directions. This, to my way of thinking, was a danger, for if the enemy had contact with any spies or fifth columnists in Padang, as he undoubtedly had, then news of our pending departure would quickly reach him and another ship would be added to Davy Jones' Locker, to say nothing of passengers and crew. We may have been over sensitive about these things, and the Colonel may have had some reason, unknown to us, for refusing this information; anyhow, let it be here said that during the day we had contact with him he was charming and helpful and—it is a very big 'and'—he was staying behind himself to do anything more he could. He was, I think, an Irishman from Cork.

After a longish walk and much hesitation we reached the station. On the way Sid wandered off the road thinking he had found something which looked like a station, and I was unreasonably alarmed when I missed him. I shouted and called him for some time without answer and ran up and down in a state of nerves looking for him. It was really very foolish, for Sid was well able to look after himself, but I was immensely relieved when he turned up. We had helped each other throughout and nothing could have been worse than to lose him at this stage.

We all arrived at the station long before the train was due to leave, and tired men threw themselves down on the cold platform to sleep. It was a ghostly scene at that railway station, with figures moving about here and there with packs on their backs seeking somewhere to rest, and when the unlighted train moved slowly into position the feeling of unreality was increased. Fortunately, the moon was now shining and we had light with which to entrain if there was none in the train itself.

During the twenty minutes' journey the train made all the noises it knew. The whistle was blown almost continuously, and again it seemed to us the height of folly to advertise our departure in that way. Surely the utmost secrecy was desirable, and instead we might have been going to a fair. Perhaps our nerves were giving out. Anyhow, by the time we reached the quayside we were as good as sunk in our own minds. At the station there was any number of natives about and, horror of horrors, there were bright lights burning. If we could not command a sinking we had at least deserved it.

CHAPTER FOURTEEN

A BRIEF OUTLINE

THE READER WILL REMEMBER that upwards of a thousand people left Singapore on the evening of February the 13th on the four ships, *Kuala, Tien Kwang, Grasshopper,* and *Dragonfly,* yet there were only about fifty at Padang with us, and a number of those had not been on any of the above ships. In order to show clearly what happened to the rest of the passengers and to others who escaped by different ships and boats I propose to devote this chapter to a brief summary, so far as I know it, of the ways and means by which people tried to escape from Malaya, and the success or failure which attended their efforts.

A glance at the map will show that the tapering peninsula which is Malaya peters out at Singapore; but due south, at no great distance, is the Rhiow archipelago, consisting of many islands, some a fair size but mostly too small to be shown distinctly on an average map. None of these islands is completely developed; villages exist at various points on the coasts of the larger ones, and on a small one here and there is a little village or kampong. Many of them are completely uninhabited, and all are thickly covered with jungle. The straits which run between and around them are mostly swift-flowing currents infested with sharks and other objectionable inhabitants of the seas. These islands lie on the straight line between Singapore and Batavia.

To the west of the whole of Malaya and also of the Rhiow Archipelago lies the large island of Sumatra. As sea routes go Sumatra is a comparatively short distance away, and this fact, combined with others, made escape from Malaya *via* Sumatra the obvious route, especially if only small craft were available. During the campaign on the peninsula many troops got cut off from their units, and some of them, reaching the west coast, found launches, sail-boats, and row-boats, and pushed out westwards in these. Those who were not captured or lost at sea landed on Sumatra and, as this was fairly early on, had little difficulty in crossing that country and finding a ship at one of the west coast ports. A few who managed this were taken to Java, but the more fortunate went to Australia, India or Ceylon.

The position in Northern Sumatra in early February is some what obscure, but by the time Singapore Island was invaded it must have been almost impossible to get from Malaya to Northern Sumatra, because the Japanese had complete control of the intervening sea and air. Sumatra was, to all intents and purposes, undefended, and from the Japanese point of view there was nothing to do but walk in. Almost certainly they had, at this time, control of the northern coasts if they had not yet occupied the whole of the northern area. This being so, escapees were now making for the more southerly parts of Sumatra and for Java. When I talk about escapees I refer to those who were escaping from Japanese occupied Malaya and those who were making a last-minute attempt to leave Singapore. Many women and children and some few men advanced in years who had left Singapore on or before February the 11th in ocean-going ships had mostly got to British territory *via* the Sunda Straits between Sumatra and Java, or to Java itself, and crossing that country to the west had picked up ships on the Indian Ocean side. The *Kuala* and the other ships which left Singapore tried, as the reader knows, to get to Batavia but, for some time, that had been becoming increasingly difficult for, in addition to the danger from attack immediately south of Singapore, Batavia was under constant observation and had been subject to frequent air raids, while enemy submarines were in all the seas. Borneo and Celebes had been in Japanese hands for some time.

If we rule out Batavia as a landing-place from, say, the February 13th, then the only possible line of escape was *via* central or southern Sumatra. As Palembang was occupied on February the 15th and the whole of the southern part of Sumatra shortly afterwards, there remained only a corridor, across the central part of the island not yet in Japanese hands. As a result of this, those who left Singapore just before or just after the city fell, including those who were cast upon the islands of the Rhiow Archipelago, tried to make their escape across this corridor. News was, of course, difficult to get; and many, thinking that other parts of Sumatra were still free, walked into captivity by landing in the north or south parts of the island. The happy chance which left this corridor was due to Japanese pre-occupation elsewhere. The battle of Java was on, and the enemy were concentrating all their attention on that. Sumatra was of little strategic value, and with Java gone it could be had for the asking, so the Japanese elected to occupy it more leisurely. Being a very large territory little opened up, obviously there was no object in alienating many troops until the main objective of Java had been dealt with. To those crossing the corridor, time was all important, as it was impossible to say when the enemy would turn his attention to it, and then it would only be a matter of days or even hours until all Sumatra would be completely under his domination.

People were leaving Singapore and reaching Sumatra even after the city had fallen. There was more than one route across the corridor; for example, some used the Siak River instead of the Indragiri as we had, and many, perhaps, used no river at all, but crossed on land from coast to coast.

The refugees who got to Sumatra from the mainland of Malaya comparatively early in the campaign were, in all probability, the forerunners of the organization which we found in operation in central Sumatra. Word may even have got back from them to Singapore before the end, for certain it was that the knowledge that such a route existed was fairly common by the time the capitulation took place. Some who left Singapore, not knowing where they were going, received news of this route in many strange ways. Posted up prominently in a village on at least one island was a large notice giving directions to refugees as to how they should make good their escape by this established route.

Although the quickest and most direct way of escape was across the sea straight from Malaya to Sumatra, many, not knowing this, or fearing the long open sea voyage in small craft, chose to go south first through the Rhiow Strait, and these joined up with the survivors of the *Kuala* and the other ships. It was fortunate for the survivors that this was so, for these men in their boats rendered many a service collecting and transporting people who otherwise might have been stuck on the islands.

When the *Kuala, Tien Kwang, Grasshopper,* and *Dragonfly* were sunk survivors were cast on many islands considerable distances apart. Broadly speaking, it is safe to say that all those who found themselves on islands other than Pompong eventually passed through Sinajang or Dabo, and got to the mainland of Sumatra. Those on Pompong, by far the greatest number, got away by a variety of means. Two small parties each in a lifeboat went off on their own and reached the mainland safely. The *Tanjong Pinang* took off some hundred and eighty women and children and about twenty wounded; but she, according to the latest information, was captured in the Java Sea. A motor trawler made two voyages from Sumatra to the island and took off some more women and wounded on the first occasion, and on the second trip took the last of the 'islanders' away. These included most of the P.W.D. officers, some civilians, and at least one woman, Mrs. Nunn.

Between the trawler's first and second trip a few got away on small native boats, as we did, and followed our route to the main land, but more than half of all who had originally been on Pompong left in Chinese tongkangs at or about the same time as the trawler made her last departure. These tongkangs, after a voyage very trying to the passengers, arrived at Dabo. It had been considered that they were not suitable boats to attempt the trip straight to Sumatra.

When the trawler left the island the first time she promised to return, but before she got back the three tongkangs arrived. I have heard conflicting stories of how the selection was made of those who were to go on the tongkangs and of those who were to await the trawler, but the truth seems to be as follows: The men in charge on the island decided that the Services must stay together and, as the trawler was too small to take them all, they were detailed to the tongkangs. In the same way it was agreed that the P.W.D. contingent should await the trawler. The civilians and the women were given the choice as to whether they would go by the tongkangs which were there or wait for the faster trawler which, if she arrived, would head straight for Sumatra. Some chose one, some the other; and just after the choice had been made the trawler appeared. It was then ruled that the choice, as made, must be adhered to, although the trawler and the tongkangs would now sail about the same time. In consequence, those who chose to await the trawler landed in Sumatra a long time before the passengers on the tongkangs, for the latter were landed at Dabo, and had to wait for other transport to take them from there to the mainland across open sea. All those who went by the trawler on her first or second trips got quickly across Sumatra and got away from the west coast, although it is feared some of them lost their lives between Sumatra and Colombo. The others who went by the tongkangs joined, at Dabo, survivors who had been on islands other than Pompong, and both lots eventually managed to leave that place. Unfortunately a few went from Dabo to Jambi rather than to the Indragiri River, and they were caught by the Japanese. The great majority, however, used the Indragiri, and got to Ayer Moleh. It was at this latter place that some seven hundred were unable to get further for some time on account of the lack of transport; they also were eventually captured by the Japanese.

All the time this was going on individuals and small parties who had escaped from Singapore in row-boats, sail-boats, and launches were making their way by devious routes from landing spots on the east of Sumatra to the clearing port of Padang on the west coast. A number who left Padang with us had come to be there in this fashion, and had not, as I have said, been on any of the bombed ships.

As the lists compiled at Padang have not been sent out, it is impossible for me to say how many in all got as far as Padang and left for British territory, nor is it possible to say how many were lost after leaving Padang. It is, however, more than likely that of all those who left Singapore in our cluster of ships only about one hundred and thirty reached freedom, and some hundred of these were people who left Pompong on the trawler which made two trips to the island. We were, I believe, the last to leave Sumatra and get through; for extensive enquiries which I have made have failed to establish that any behind us ever reached free territory. I am constantly asked how many British civilians were left behind in Singapore itself, and my guess is between eight and nine thousand men and between two and three hundred women. This is only a guess, but I will be surprised if it is not approximately correct. It is comforting to know that what meagre information there is at the moment (July 1942) indicates that they are being treated well.

CHAPTER FIFTEEN

IN GOD'S HAND

I WILL NEVER FORGET my first glimpse of the Ss. *Palopo,* although really there was nothing extraordinary about her. A small freighter, she had escaped at the last moment from Java and called in at Emmerhaven to get fuel. Signs of hasty coaling were evident, for her decks were covered inches thick in coal grit and dust and, when we first boarded her, this is what we spread our blanket on before lying down. Except a few cabins for the ship's officers there was no accommodation whatever other than the deck, hatches, and galley-ways. The *Palopo* carried no armament at all, had no wireless, and was still uncamouflaged. In case of attack our only hope lay in the lifeboats and the cork lifebelts with which we were provided.

When, in the afternoon, we arranged to go on her, we expected that she would sail shortly after dark or at least before midnight, but as time went on we recognized that there was no chance of that. We then thought that she would sail as soon as we got on board, possibly about four o'clock. This worried us because it only left two hours till dawn and about five or six till the reconnaissance plane might be expected to come over. In this ship we could not get far away in that time, and the chances of being seen were great. Even the warships, which had left Padang days and weeks earlier, and consequently at much less dangerous times, had sailed a lot earlier in the night than that and had, with their superior speed, been able to put many more miles than we could hope to do between themselves and land before the danger hour arrived. The plane which we dreaded was accustomed to fly over the town and along the coast every morning between nine and ten-thirty searching for victims, and, seemingly, our only chance of escaping detection was to be out of sight by then.

We did get on board about four, but the ship did not sail immediately. Half-past four came, then five, then half-past five, and still we lay alongside. It is easy to judge our consternation at this delay; it seemed like throwing our chances away, and if we had had the courage of our convictions no doubt some of us would have gone back on shore again to face capture rather than another aerial attack which, to those left alive, would mean capture anyway.

I did not see the captain in the early hours of that morning, but I noticed the mate looking anxiously at his watch and at the sky as it brightened in the east towards six o'clock. I asked him at what time we were leaving, and he, a man of many words as we afterwards found out, replied monosyllabically, "Six." And six it was.

It is perhaps true that a coward dies a thousand deaths against the brave man's one, but it is also true that when danger against which one has no weapon is present, it is only the stupid man who does not realize it and fear it unless he has finished with life, but that does not mean that he shows fear; in most cases the opposite is the case, he is outwardly calm and collected. No one showed fear on this ship, but I would wager a lot that every mind was possessed of a deep apprehension as to our fate, enhanced, no doubt, by the experiences of the past few weeks or months.

Much has been written and said about what men think of

when faced with death or deadly peril, and I suppose the answer is, as it is to so many questions, 'It depends on the man'. I find it difficult to remember what I thought of in the preceding months during the moments of greatest immediate danger. I am afraid it was of nothing very relevant or important and, as we left Sumatra in that grey silent dawn, my thoughts were equally trivial. I know that my body was saturated with feeling, my nerves alive to every noise and movement, and my mind, as it were, thinking too much to produce thoughts. The froth of its activity alone came to the surface and crystallized into conscious forms. Foolish forms which pretended to be thoughts. Thoughts of how it would be a pity to sweep the decks as the coal dust would mar the beauty of the sea. Thoughts of how the delays in sailing had enabled us to avoid setting off on a Friday, the unlucky day for sailing, the day on which we had left Singapore. Thoughts of how every ship which went down must appear a miraculous and providential happening to the fishes and the million animals which inhabit the bottom of the oceans. Here, indeed, to them was manna from above; first, there was the exposed food for them; then gradually, as tins and doors rusted through, the products of the ends of the earth made feast after feast. Here, indeed, was a great new pleasure city where the old fish could bask and the young could play hide-and-seek and follow-my-leader from captain's cabin to passenger's commode. Nothing ever happened to man on earth to compare with this event in the lives of the fishes. It was a new world arriving out of space, colossal in form, munificent in bounty, extravagant in possibilities, and amazing in its unexpectedness. Foolish, even flippant, were my thoughts, and they did not at all interpret the workings of the mind.

Sid turned to me and said: "Either the captain's crazy or I am." Fortunately it was a statement, not a question, and it needed no answer.

Half an hour later we were told that the Colonel wanted to speak to us all on top of the front hatch. I didn't know there was a Colonel on board, but evidently such was the case, and he had taken it upon himself to be our leader. We all assembled for'ard, and a small, thin, obviously unassuming man appeared at a level above us. For a seemingly long time he stood in silence as though embarrassed and undecided what to say, and then, of all things in the world, he said "Good morning", and smiled. If he had said "Shun" or "Prepare to meet thy God" or even "Heil", I think we would have remained unmoved, but "Good morning" was too much for us. I am afraid we laughed, not meaning to be rude, but at that moment they were the last words we expected to hear. The Colonel went on to say that the ship's captain expected the journey to Colombo to last for six or seven days; he had enough food to give us three meals a day, there would not be much variety, but we were all refugees, and could do with what there was. There was sufficient water if we used it sparingly, and the captain hoped to allot us a bathroom and some hot water—more laughter. There were only four lifeboats, two on each side, and if the ship was hit two of them would undoubtedly be destroyed, so one of those remaining was to be reserved for the officers and crew, and the other was to be put at our disposal. The captain had said that he thought the Japanese usually gave warning before they sank a ship, but, added the Colonel, "we have been lucky so far, and we will get through all right." We cheered him.

Afterwards, on the deck, I had a talk with the Colonel, and among other things he said, "We can take no account of to-morrow, the miraculous has already happened; here we are on a ship bound for Colombo, who would believe it?" Well, this man might say that the miraculous had happened, for he was Lieut.-Colonel A. E. Cumming, whose story is told in this cutting from the *Times of Ceylon:*

V.C. HERO'S SURPRISE

HEARD OF AWARD ONLY TO-DAY

Lieut.-Colonel A. E Cumming, of the Third Battalion 2/12 Frontier Force Regiment, received a surprise in Colombo to-day. He discovered that he had been awarded the V.C.

Lieut.-Colonel Cumming had fought his way with his regiment through some of the thickest fighting in Malaya, been wounded about seven times, and had escaped from Singapore.

He told a Times of Ceylon reporter to-day that he was, till to-day, unaware that he had been awarded the V.C., and for what particular incident in the fighting. His first intimation of the award was when an officer in Ceylon gave him a copy of an illustrated magazine announcing the distinction conferred on him.

"We fought on the north-west border of Malaya," he said, "and then fought a rear-guard action down south. The thickest fighting was perhaps in Kuantan and in Kelantan, where the regiment was very hard pressed. The Japanese attacked in swarms, and we killed a large number of them. The bitterest time we had was in guarding a landing-ground in Kuantan, where the regiment was badly knocked about."

Lieut.-Colonel Cumming received two bayonet wounds in the stomach during the fighting and several bullet wounds, and was in a base hospital for some time. Just after he

*recovered he was placed in command of the Jat Regiment in
Singapore, which also fought magnificently to the end.*

HAZARDOUS ESCAPE

*Lieut.-Colonel Cumming and eleven other British officers
hid themselves and watched Japanese movements in the
island. They boarded a Chinese junk in which they hid for
three days. They then went to an island nearby and spent two
days there till they were able to buy two sampans for three
hundred dollars.*

*They set out in the sampans, but were wrecked in a storm
near the Sultan Shoal lighthouse. Three of them then went
across in a small boat to the Raffles lighthouse on another
island, where they found a strong rowing-boat. With the aid
of the lighthouse-keeper there they rigged up a mast and sail
and, with the twelve others, escaped towards Sumatra.*

*Lieut.-Colonel Cumming picked up an old Dutch map
which served as their guide. On their way to Sumatra, a
Japanese plane sighted the boat and machine-gunned them.
One of the officers was shot through both legs. That night they
were blown ashore on a rocky island on the east coast, where
the wounded officer had to be left behind. They then
contacted the Dutch authorities in Sumatra, who helped
them to escape.*

*Lieut.-Colonel Cumming was awarded the M.C. in the last
world war during the fighting in Palestine.*

During the morning we all kept an anxious watch on the
skies. Never had land been so long in disappearing, never
had a ship seemed to go so slowly. We found that the
Palopo's speed was less even than we had expected; she
could only do about nine knots, and Sid and I made endless

mental calculations about where she would be at ten o'clock-when the Japanese plane was bound to be on the search—and about the distances one could see from an aeroplane at such and such a height. Together with others we restlessly paced the deck, eyes ever turning towards the distant sky, where the Sumatran coast lay below it. If nothing happened before one o'clock we might get away with it, but it was a long time till one o'clock, and the hours dragged so. Midday passed, and the coast faded below the horizon, and nothing became it like the leaving of it. I think we were lucky; I think we were very, very lucky. It was a cloudy day and surely this saved us. If the Japanese had kept to their usual routine, and there was no reason to doubt it, the plane would have come and gone by now, and that was indeed encouraging, so much so that Potts remarked to an anxious pacer of the deck, "Man, there is a God above us," and it takes a lot of encouragement to make Potts say that.

At five in the evening we came to some islands and dropped anchor till dark. We were about to go into the Siberat Straits, and the captain wanted to go through in the dark, for it was known to be a favourite lurking-place for submarines which hoped to catch shipping in these narrow waters. Having been up all the night before I was dead-beat and lay down. I stayed awake just long enough to realize that we were zig-zagging in approved fashion, and then sleep overcame me. The next thing I heard was the mate's voice talking to a man close to me; the voice was tinged with relief, and he was evidently in high spirits. We were through the Straits and still afloat. He went below and brought up a blanket for someone, and in reply to the thanks he said, "We must all help each other and then everything will be all right." Spoken in an attractive foreign accent in the dark of the night it was a peculiarly impressive statement. I went to sleep again, repeating "We must all help each other"; "We must all help each other, then everything will be all right"; "We must all help—"

Sometimes when travelling in foreign countries far from home and sleeping in different places every night I have found, on awakening, difficulty in realizing exactly where I was. It is a curious sensation when, after a minute or so, it dawned on me that I was in Jasper, Rotorua, Nikko, Wengen, Sien-Reap, Taxaco, Suva or San Antonio. On this voyage I awoke with a somewhat similar feeling of uncertainty, but it was uncertainty of a different kind. I wondered for a vague minute or so if I was really alive or in another world; everything seemed so peaceful and, possibly due to the weeks of thin living, my body seemed somehow distant.

We had been warned that there would not be much variety in the food. Well, we had potatoes, ducks' eggs, bread and rice. The former two appeared once or twice, and the latter two at every meal. Rice and bread were, to all intents and purposes, what we lived on, but they were dished out in fairly liberal helpings three times a day. We were always ready for them, in fact eager for them. As there were not enough plates to go round, everyone did not get helped in the first rush, and the less fortunate men each selected a victim and hung around near him until he had finished, urging him to eat quickly so that the plate might become available. Table manners were, I am afraid, at a discount; we grabbed and gulped, and went away showing our dissatisfaction at the monotony of the diet, not that we had forgotten how lucky we were, but because food had become an obsession, and we longed for something more satisfying. "What would you like for breakfast?" someone would ask sarcastically, and in grim humour the reply would be, "Rice, one might as well have everything on the menu."

The days were long and weary; there was nothing whatever to do. No work, no books, no games, not even anywhere to sit except the hard deck; but, as you were, there must have been a chair on board, for I remember someone dragged it with a scraping noise across the deck and we all jumped at the unaccustomed sound. Anything which varied the chug-chug of the engine made us start: our nerves were completely on edge. The engines suddenly stopped one evening, and we all jumped up and rushed wildly to see what was happening. We feared the worst; it must be a submarine.

It was Monday evening, and we had been almost three days at sea. As a good many miles now lay between us and the land we had begun to look on the possibilities of air attack as negligible, and had cheered up in consequence. Our cheerfulness was to receive a blow, for the ship had stopped to pick up two Malay seamen from a raft which the millionth chance had brought across our path. Their story was that they had been employed as stokers on a ship carrying many evacuee passengers from Padang. In the middle of the night they were torpedoed and the ship sank in five minutes. When daylight came these two men were alone among the wreckage, both clinging to kapok floats. They came together, and by using pieces of wood found floating around and strips from their clothing they were able to construct a rough raft on which they sat half submerged. That was nine days previously, and they had had nothing to eat and only rain-water to drink, which they collected in cupped hands from the odd showers. Tossed about in the middle of the Indian Ocean they had survived nine days of this existence till by the grace of Allah we nearly rammed them. No boat was lowered to bring them in; instead, ropes were thrown to which they clung and were dragged on board.

The effect of this story on us can be imagined. The cheerfulness which had begun to bloom rapidly died, and the ship was once again in profound gloom. We were divided up into parties and set to watch for submarines. Perhaps this was a good thing, as it gave us something to do, and made us feel that no precaution was being neglected; but, in fact, it was very useless, for even if a submarine was spotted early there was nothing we could possibly do without guns and with no speed.

It was just about here that an incident of which I was told later happened to one party of evacuees. The party was on board a Chinese river-boat escaping from Java when a submarine appeared and fired two torpedoes, which came straight for the boat. What an awful moment it must have been as the passengers watched the torpedoes coming straight for them with no time to get out of the way. The torpedoes, however, passed right below the shallow draught boat and could be seen continuing their journey on the other side. After firing the torpedoes the submarine disappeared and, before it rose to the surface again some little distance off, the passengers, with great presence of mind, had rigged up a spar to look like a gun and made great pretence of aiming and preparing to fire with this make-believe weapon. The submarine was deceived, or else she had no more torpedoes or was too astonished at seeing the boat still afloat to continue the attack, for she submerged again, reappeared about a mile away, and then finally made off.

I have mentioned the twelve civilians who were on this ship, but there were also others whom we had met before.

Company Sergeant-Major Flannigan was on board; he had left Singapore in a row-boat and been thirteen days at sea before he got other assistance. The singing 'cook' of the *Kingfisher* was there also, and still singing. Someone asked him what he had to sing about when he only got rice to eat, and his reply, if I remember aright, was: "When a man is happy in his heart he sings, is it not so?"

Major Kellett we had not met before. A doctor in the R.A.M.C., he dressed all our sores from a very scanty store of medical supplies. Of the others new to us the officers were mostly in Colonel Cumming's party, and the rankers were drawn from many units of the Services.

Brewer's leg got worse. He was allotted one of the few cabins, and stayed there most of the time. Sid also suffered a lot, and as for the rest of us, our wounds did not improve. We tried to freshen ourselves up with the odd shave, one razor shearing many beards, and washed what clothes we had with a scanty supply of water and severely rationed soap. On the whole, even apart from the danger, the days were very miserable and dreary, and when it rained we were wretched, for there was little cover and we usually got wet.

The rain at night was worst. Sid and I slept on iron plates on top of the coal bunker in front of the funnel. There was a ragged canvas awning overhead, but it leaked badly and the rain poured through it, so we had to get up, go below, and stand in the galley ways till it chose to stop. It often took a long time to stop.

On the whole, however, the weather was fine, but in a ship likely to be torpedoed or bombed one's view of the weather is somewhat different from what it is on a pleasure trip. Bad weather, so to speak, is good weather, because it reduces the possibilities of attack; thus our fine weather was not much to our liking. The moon also was less welcome than it normally is, for at sea, in war time, the moon is a menace. In those days it was very bright, and I remember doing a submarine watch from four to six o'clock in the morning when it was at its most brilliant. There were many clouds in the sky, and I always thought and hoped that in a minute or two they would obscure it; but somehow they always seemed to avoid it, missing it by inches or melting away before they reached it. It was most annoying but lovely to watch, as big clouds and little clouds took on their momentary glow and passed into darkness.

I don't know whether we liked the day or the night least, I think we welcomed both as a change in the monotony of the trip. We watched the great red ball arise in the east and the green flash as the sun went down with equal dislike, and all we wished for was that the period between the two would lessen. Time couldn't pass too quickly. In the periods of supreme happiness one wishes time to stand still, and the intensity of one's happiness or misery can be measured by the rate at which we wish the clock to go round.

The mate sometimes entertained us with his conversation, and he always had a ready audience. A very corpulent man, he had both a humorous and a biting tongue. He had many hard things to say about the Malayan campaign and our conduct of it and, apparently under the impression that the British considered the Dutch a secondary Power in the East, he rubbed in all the Dutch had done and somewhat minimized the exploits of the British, though it was all in good part. He pointed out rightly that the Dutch in the Netherlands East Indies were the only Power—apart from France and ourselves at the start—who had declared war before they were attacked. Immediately on the outbreak of war in the East they had thrown their lot in with us and given all they had. His favourite theme was that we were no longer able to look on ourselves as supermen; we must get down to it if we were to come out on top.

The sixth day after we left Sumatra was Friday, March the 13th. Danger makes men superstitious, and we did not look with favour on a Friday, especially if it was the 13th. During this voyage men talked often of what they would do when they arrived in Colombo, but Colombo was never mentioned without the touching of wood. Among groups of men standing here and there a figure would stoop and touch the deck now and then, and it was easy to tell someone had said 'when we reach Colombo'. Lest some strong man be annoyed, I hasten to add that there may have been among us some who were not superstitious, some scientists who would not stoop to touching wood or some Christian who put his faith in a Greater Power. Certain it is that the army still has its Ironsides, for I saw a soldier reading his Bible every evening before sundown. Friday, March the 13th was not unlucky, but it was momentous.

A few hours after breakfast three ships were sighted heading across our course; there was no possibility of avoiding them. It had been my experience in this war that all passenger and cargo ships on the high seas avoid contact with any other ship if they can. No sooner is a ship sighted than they turn away and get out of sight as quickly as possible. The other ship may be an enemy vessel. How different it was in peace-time, when the meeting of another ship was an event looked forward to when sailing far from land, another friendly human contact in a waste of seas.

The three ships became more distinct, and soon it was apparent that one of them, at least—the leading one—was a ship-of-war. She detached herself from the others and headed towards us. The captain and mate on the bridge were busy with telescopes, and we waited breathlessly for some sign from them as to what we might expect. After a little while the mate came down and spoke to us. "Gentlemen," he said, "we have brought you close to the shores of Ceylon. We can do no more; you are now in God's hand. If she is a British ship all is well; if she is the enemy—" And he shrugged his shoulders.

After a tense period of waiting, signals flashed between us and then she turned away. Were we relieved?—to borrow an Americanism, I'll say we were.

The warship had not left without a warning, however; we were still in submarine-haunted waters, no vigilance must be relaxed. In spite of that we were uplifted by contact with a British ship: it felt more like home; surely nothing could get us now. The mate said cheerfully, "You have now only two hundred miles to swim."

The day passed without further incident, and Sid and I lay down on our iron plate that last night just as we had done on previous nights, but there was a difference: we were filled with hope. In the morning our hope was justified, the shores of Ceylon were in sight. How good it was to see them!

Ever so slowly, it seemed, we got nearer and nearer, and at last our arrival was a certainty.

We steamed up between the guiding rows of buoys until a few hundred yards outside the breakwater, and there dropped anchor. We four shook hands all round, and I said to Sid, "We have made it"; to which he replied, "When you said in the President's room 'it will be an adventure' you little thought how true it would be."

A pilot-boat came close by and the pilot shouted, "What ship?"

"The *Palopo*." "Any refugees?" "Yes."

"Are you short of food?" A chorus answered, "Yes."

"We are very full up," he shouted; "you may not get in till to-morrow morning, but I'll try to get you in to-night! In the meantime you are in the fairway, move up behind that ship with three funnels."

He passed on, and a howl of disapproval went up from all of us. To think that we had gone through that voyage and much else to be kept waiting twenty-four hours outside Colombo Harbour. The iniquity of it! We were getting 'uppish', I am afraid, and one Oxford accent was heard saying, "To think he called us refugees. I hope I have the chance of not standing that man a drink."

The lifeboats were raided to furnish our midday meal, for other stocks had run out. The afternoon dragged along till after four o'clock, when someone took pity on us and another pilot came along and took us into the harbour. We had arrived; and I, for one, felt undyingly grateful to Captain Bosman, his jovial mate, the engineers, officers, and crew of the good ship *Palopo* which had brought us through great hazards, real and imaginary. Only those who have sailed the seas in war-time can know our debt to the merchant seamen of all the United Nations.

Safe in the harbour we expected to be taken off with all haste and received with open arms. But no; there was nothing chancy like that about the administration of a British port. We had to wait for the doctor to examine us; that took some time. We had to wait for the police to examine us, and they did not turn up till nearly dark, and then informed us that we could not get off until the emigration people had come aboard, taken a list of our names and references back to the land, and put them before a committee. By this time we were getting desperate. I think we would have swum and smuggled ourselves ashore before we would have faced another night on that boat. Sir John Bagnall followed and spoke to one of the police officers, but coming back said, "We may think we are big men, but to them we are just another lot of refugees."

Somehow our advent must have become known ashore, for out of the dark, amid heavy rain, came a launch which drew up along side. Captain J. Pye, of the European Association, came aboard and said, in effect, "Come along with me." We all piled into his launch. How he side-tracked the regulations I do not know, but at that moment we could have fallen on his neck in gratitude. In a few minutes we stepped ashore on British soil.

Sid and Brewer went to hospital immediately, and Potts was billeted on some kindly people. I drove with Mr. Douglas Simpson, my wife's cousin, to his house in the suburbs— where he and his wife killed the fatted calf on my behalf.

A warm bath, a good dinner, and I went to bed; but the bed was too comfortable to allow me to sleep at once. I lay awake and thought. I thought of the future for the first time: What was I to do now? Where was my place in the world? I thought also of the recent past and of all that had happened. Chance, Fate or Providence, call it what you will, I had surely been very fortunate; how easily it might have been otherwise. If I had been a few yards this way or that many times during the bombing and shelling of Singapore, if I had feared taking the last-minute outside chance, if I had been at a different part of the *Kuala* when she was hit, if I had been unable to swim, or if I had had a lifebelt and been unable to submerge, if there had been no friendly rock when I was halfway up the hill, if I had left Pompong by another boat, if I had drunk foul water or got sick, if Sid and I had not made a push for it at Ayer Moleh, if we had taken the bus instead of the car at Pekan Bharu, if we had hesitated at Padang, or even perhaps if the

Palopo had taken a slightly different route I would now have been dead or captured. If any one of a dozen things had been otherwise than it was I could never have told this story. It seemed indeed, that I had been fortunate. But had I? How does a man assess his fortune? Of what does a man's wealth consist? Not long before I had a good job, considerable savings, a pleasant house well provided with furnishings and effects—including a treasured collection of books, an irreplaceable magazine of coloured films taken in many parts of the world, and all the usual valued things one gathers in half a lifetime. So far as I knew all were lost: job, money, treasures, records and papers, and of all that I had in Singapore there remained to me now only ragged shorts and shirt, broken canvas shoes, my identity disc, my passport, and my wallet containing a Dutch guilder, an identity card, my pass to leave Singapore, and a blurred snapshot of my wife and child; yet, that night I thanked God as I had never done before for all that was left: for life, freedom, family, friends, the health and the will to start again.

Appendix A: Escaped and Lost

[*The following lists were compiled some time after the events related in the book, and the author does not vouch for their accuracy. The lists are also far from complete.*]

POMPONG

People at Pompong or lost when the *Kuala* and *Tien Kwang* were sunk.

Names	Address/Occupation	Fate
Miss Allen	Nursing Sister	?
Miss Beattie	Nursing Sister	Escaped
Miss Bell-Murray	Q.A.I.N.S.	Escaped
Miss Brebner	Singapore	On *Tanjong Pinang*
Mrs. F. W. Brewer	Singapore	On *Tanjong Pinang*
Miss Brooks	(Unknown)	Believed Lost
Miss Jean Brown	(Unknown)	?
Mrs. C. R. Cherry	Singapore	?
Mrs. D. Crawford	Johore	Believed Lost
Dr. (Miss) Crow	Singapore	Reached Sumatra
Dr. (Miss) Craig	(Unknown)	Died at Dabo
Miss Craig	(Unknown)	On *Tanjong Pinang*
Mrs. Doughty	Kuala Lumpur	Reached Sumatra
Miss Doughty	Kuala Lumpur	Reached Sumatra
Miss Doughty	Kuala Lumpur	?
Miss G. Dowling	Q.A.I.N.S.	Escaped
Miss P. Evans	Q.A.I.N.S.	?
Miss Franklin	Nursing Sister	?

Mrs. R. H. Green ... Singapore.......On *Tanjong Pinang*
Miss Giffen .... Singapore.......................?
Miss Hardie........ Seremban.......................?
Miss Harding ...... Singapore.......................?
Mra. Hawes........ Port Dickson..... Reached Sumatra
Mrs. Hill .... Singapore............Believed Lost
Mrs. Hulf.......... (Unknown) .... Escaped
Miss Hurst......... (Unknown) ....Believed Lost
Mrs. Jacques .... Taiping.........On *Tanjong Pinang*
Dr. (Miss) Jones .... (Unknown) ....?
Miss Jones .... Singapore.......................?
Mrs. Colin King .... (Unknown) .....On *Tanjong Pinang*
Mrs. Kitchen .... Singapore.......On *Tanjong Pinang*
Miss Key .... Penang ....?
Mrs. Leggatt .... (Unknown) .... Escaped
Miss Logan .... (Unknown) ....Believed Lost
Dr. (Miss) Lyon..... Johore Bharu..... Reached Sumatra
Miss Macdonald.... Singapore................ Escaped
Mr's. Marshall...... Singapore.......................?
Mrs. McDuff....... Ipok ....?
Mrs. McIntyre...... Singapore.......................?
Mrs. W. McMullen.. Batu Pahat................ Escaped
Miss Milne......... (Unknown) .....On *Tanjong Pinang*
Miss Moore........ (Unknown) ....?
Dr. (Miss) Morris ... Kuala Lumpur............ Escaped
Mrs. R. L. Nunn .... Singapore............Believed Lost
Mrs. Pattara........ (Unknown) ....?
Miss Pattara........ (Unknown) ....?
Miss Pattara........ (Unknown) ....?
Miss Pattara........ Singapore.......On *Tanjong Pinang*
Mrs. A. C. Potts .... Singapore.......On *Tanjong Pinang*
Mrs. Prentis........ (Unknown) ....Believed Lost
Mrs. Robertson..... Singapore.......On *Tanjong Pinang*
Madame Ruperties.. Singapore.......................?

Miss Scott . . . . (Unknown) . . . . .On *Tanjong Pinang*
Mrs. Sherlow. . . . . . . Klang . . . .?
Miss Sims. . . . . (Unknown) . . . . Believed lost
Miss Sloan . . . . Penang . . . . Escaped
Miss Smith. . . . . Singapore. . . . .?
Miss Speading. . . . . . (Unknown) . . . .?
Mrs. Stafford . . . . Taiping . . . . .On *Tanjong Pinang*
Mrs. E. G. Staunton . Singapore. . . . . .Believed Lost
Mrs. Stevens . . . . (Unknown) . . . .?
Mrs. Tate . . . . Singapore. . . . . . .On *Tanjong Pinang*
Mrs. Thomson. . . . . . Singapore. . . . . . .On *Tanjong Pinang*
Dr. (Miss) Thompson . .(Unknown) . . . .?
Mrs. Watts-Carter . . Sitiawan . . . .?
Mrs. Williams . . . . . . Malacca . . . .?
Miss Wright. . . . . (Unknown) . . . . . .On *Tanjong Pinang*

Mr. Anderson . . . . . . P.W.D. Escaped
Mr. Amery. . . . . P.W.D. Escaped
Mr. Aste . . . . Mercantile Bank . . . .?
Mr. Bagbie . . . . P.W.D. Escaped
Mr. Bell . . . . F.M.S.R. . . . .?
Mr. W. O. Belton. . . . P.W.D. Escaped
Mr. F. D. Bisseker . . . (Unknown) . . . .?
Mr. Borman. . . . . P.W.D. Escaped
Mr. Bossier . . . . P.W.D. Escaped
Mr. Braddley . . . . P.W.D. Escaped
Capt. W. Briggs . . . . . Ship's Master . . . .?
Mr. W. D. Brown. . . . Chartered Bank. . . . .?
Mr. Burke-Gaffney . . P.W.D. Escaped
Mr. Bruce-Smith. . . . P.W.D. Escaped
Mr. Burton. . . . . P.W.D. Escaped
Mr. Bryan . . . . P.W.D. Escaped
Capt. Caithness. . . . . Ship's Master . . . .?
Mr. Cambridge . . . . . P.W.D. Escaped

Mr. R. D. Campbell . P.W.D.................... Escaped
Mr. Campbell ...... P.W.D..................... Escaped
Mr. Cartwright ..... P.W.D..................... Escaped
Mr. F. G. Coales .... P.W.D...................... Killed
Mr. C. Cox. .... Singapore.......................?
Mr. Davies. .... F.M.S.R. ....?
Mr. D. J. Davis...... P.W.D..........................?
Mr. E. R. Davis ..... P.W.D..........................?
Mr. Davidson ...... P.W.D..................... Escaped
Mr. Dibden .... P.W.D..................... Escaped
Mr. Dimmock...... P.W.D..................... Escaped
Mr. Fallows .... P.W.D................Believed Lost
Sg. Ld. Farewell..... R.A.F. .... Reached Sumatra
Mr. Forgin. .... P.W.D..................... Escaped
Mr. Gardiner....... P.W.D..................... Escaped
Mr. O. W. Gilmour .. Singapore Municipality .... Escaped
Mr. Grant.......... Taiping................... Escaped
Mr. Graham........ P.W.D..................... Escaped
Mr. Halliday .... P.W.D..................... Escaped
Mr. Hamilton ...... Chartered Bank...................?
Mr. Hartley and two boys ... (Unknown) ....?
Mr. Hember........ P.W.D..................... Escaped
Mr. Honiwell....... Singapore................ Escaped
Mr. Horseley .... P.W.D..................... Escaped
Mr. Husband....... P.W.D..................... Escaped
Mr. Hulton......... P.W.D..................... Escaped
Mr. A. Inglis .... P.W.D..................... Escaped
Mr. Inglis .... P.W.D..................... Escaped
Mr. R. D. Jackson ... R.A.F. ....?
Mr. Jewkes......... P.W.D..................... Escaped
Mr. S. A. Jordan .... P.W.D..................... Escaped
Mr. C. N. Joyce ..... Cable & Wireless.. Reached Sumatra
Mr. A. P. Kelly...... P.W.D..................... Escaped
Mr. S. N. Kelly...... Singapore Municipality .... Escaped

Mr. Kinlock........ Singapore......................?
Mr. L. A. Laffan...... P.W.D.................... Escaped
Mr. Lindsay........ P.W.D.................... Escaped
Mr. Mannering..... F.M.S.R. ....?
Mr. McCardle ...... Gula .... Escaped
Mr. McClure .... P.W.D.................... Escaped
Mr. McHugh .... P.W.D.................... Escaped
Mr. Mcintyre....... P.W.D.................... Escaped
Mr. P. Murphy...... P.W.D................Believed Lost
Mr. W. M. Miller.... Chartered Bank... Died in Colombo
Mr. Mitford........ P.W.D.................... Escaped
Mr. Morgan........ P.W.D.................... Escaped
Mr. Nankivel....... P.W.D.................... Escaped
Mr. R. L. Nunn ..... P.W.D................Believed Lost
Mr. O'Connell...... P.W.D.................... Escaped
Mr. R. Page .... R.R.I. ....?
Mr. G. Pape........ P.W.D.................... Escaped
Mr. Proud .... Singapore................ Escaped
Mr. Purser .... Chartered Bank..................?
Mr. A. C. Potts ..... Singapore................ Escaped
Mr. Robertson...... A.P.C. .... Reached Sumatra
Mr. I. Salmond ..... Singapore........ Reached Sumatra
Mr. Samson........ P.W.D.................... Escaped
Mr. Samuels........ Penang .... Escaped
Mr. Sawyer........ P.W.D............. Reached Sumatra
Mr. S. Scales .... Singapore................ Escaped
Mr. Scott-Ram ..... Singapore....... Reached Sumatra
Mr. Spence......... P.W.D.................... Escaped
Mr. P.H. Stevens .... P.W.D.................... Escaped
Mr. Stocks .... (Unknown) ...... Reached Sumatra
Mr. R.H. Steed ..... P.W.D.................... Escaped
Mr. H. H. Sturt ..... A.P.C. .... Reached Sumatra
Mr. R. A. Stewart ... Hong Kong Bank .... Escaped
Mr. Sutton.......... P.W.D.................... Escaped

Mr. Thatcher . . . . P.W.D. . . . . Escaped
Rev. J . R. Thomson . Singapore . . . . Escaped
Mr. E. Tongue . . . . . . Singapore . . . . .Believed Lost
Mr. Tonkin . . . . P.W.D. . . . . Escaped
Mr. Tunridge. . . . . . . P.W.D. . . . . Escaped
Mr. J. Watson. . . . . . . Perak. . . . . Escaped
Mr. A. Weir . . . . P.W.D. . . . . Escaped
Mr. Wilson . . . . Architect . . . .?
Mr. Wilson . . . . P.W.D. . . . . Escaped
Mr. E. N. C. Wollerton. .Singapore . . . . .Believed Lost
Mr. Young . . . . Planter . . . .?
Mr. Young . . . . P.W.D. . . . . Escaped

SINAJANG

Seen at Sinajang, February 19th to 22nd, 1942.

Names	Address/Occupation	Fate
S. Cunningham Brown	?	Reached Sumatra
Miss Jean Duncan	Singapore	Reached Sumatra
Mr. O. W. Gilmour	Singapore	Escaped
Mr. S. N. Kelly	Singapore	Escaped
Dr. Kirkwood	Singapore	Reached Sumatra
Mr. D. H. Kleinman	Singapore	Died at Dabo
Mrs. Moncur	?	Reached Sumatra
Dr. (Miss) Morris	Kuala Lumpur	Escaped
Mr. O'Grady	P.W.D.	Escaped
Mr. Robertson	A.P.C.	Reached Sumatra
Mr. Ross	P.W.D.	Reached Sumatra
Mr. I. Salmond	Singapore	Reached Sumatra
Mr. Samuels	Penang	Reached Sumatra
Mr. Scotts-Ram	A.P.C.	Reached Sumatra
Mr. Stocks	?	Reached Sumatra
Mr. H. H. Sturt	A.P.C.	Reached Sumatra

DABO

Seen at Dabo, February 23rd to 26th, 1942.

Names	Address/Occupation	Fate
Sir John Bagnall	Singapore	Escaped
Mr. E. J. Bennett	Singapore	Escaped
Mr. F. W. Brewer	Singapore	Escaped
Mr. E. Brown	F.M.S.R.	Reached Sumatra
Mr. Feakes	Cable & Wireless	Reached Sumatra
Mr. O. W. Gilmour	Singapore	Escaped
Mr. C. N. Joyce	Cable & Wireless	Reached Sumatra
Mr. S. N. Kelly	Singapore	Escaped
Dr. Kirkwood	Singapore	Reached Sumatra
Mr. O'Grady	P.W.D	Escaped
Mr. A. C. Potts	Singapore	Escaped
Mr. Riviere	Cable & Wireless	Reached Sumatra
Mr. Robertson	A.P.C.	Reached Sumatra
Mr. J.B. Ross	Singapore	Reached Sumatra
Mr. I. Salmond	Singapore	Reached Sumatra
Mr. Samuels	Penang	Reached Sumatra
Mr. Scoble-Nicholson	Singapore	Reached Sumatra
Mr. Scott-Ram	A.P.C.	Reached Sumatra
Mr. Smart	F.M.S.R.	Reached Sumatra
Mr. Sparrow	F.M.S.R.	Reached Sumatra
Mrs. Smart	Kuala Lumpur	Reached Sumatra
Mr. Stocks	?	Reached Sumatra
Mr. H. H. Sturt	A.P.C.	Reached Sumatra
Mr. Wagener	F.M.S.R.	Escaped

Appendix B: Captured on the Tanjong Pinang

[*The following names were broadcast from the Japanese controlled radio al Padang as being those of people captured on the* Tanjong Pinang *about February 24th, 1942.*]

Miss Helen Monia, French Palais de Modes, M.S.A., Singapore.

Mrs. Hennessey and child, wife of Lt.-Col. Hennessey, R.A.M.C.

Miss Betty Hollands and four I.M.S. girls, Indian Medical Nursing Home, Johore.

Mrs. Tate, wife of Mr. Tate, Singapore Municipality Water Department.

Mrs. Shaw, wife of Mr. Shaw, Singapore Fire Department.

Mrs. Robinson, wife of Mr. Robinson, Manager, Great Eastern Live Insurance Co.

Miss Smith, Nursing Sister, Penang.

Miss Robinson Nursing Sister, Penang.

Mrs. C. V. Staflord, Taiping.

Mrs. Llm and two children, Ipoh.

Mrs. Hartley, Pelam Estate, Kedah.

Mrs. Mather and child, Prisons Department, Kuala Lumpur.

Mrs. Jones and child, c/o Borneo Motors.

Mrs. van der Kratton and three children, Naval Base, Singapore.

Mrs. Joachim and daughter, Taiping.

Mrs. Newman and daughter, Singapore.

Miss Hilda Klassen, General Hospital, Singapore.

Mrs. Colin King, wife of Rev. Colin King.

Mrs. Somerville (husband with John Little & Co., Ltd.).

Miss E. Allan, M.A.S., Singapore.

Mr. Zehnder and four daughters, family of a Singapore lawyer.

Miss Z. de Souza, Singapore.

Miss A. Reutens, Singapore.

Mrs. Samuel, wife of Penang lawyer.

Miss Lowry, M.E.O., General Hospital.

Miss Nelson (I), M.E.O., General Hospital.

Miss E.? M. Smith, M.E.O., General Hospital.

Commander Terry, R.N. (or R.N.R.), in command of *Tanjong Pinang*.

Mrs. Collett, Collett and Whittles, Kuala Lumpur.

Mrs. Barnett, Barnett, Agricultural Department.

Mrs. Smith and four children, Bukit Timah Road, Singapore.

Mrs. Janson and two children, Serangoon Road, Singapore.

Misses Cheo and Thetie Pattara, Serangoon Road, Singapore.

Miss Wales? Dancer, Katong, Singapore.

Miss Helen Vaxaloo, Katong, Singapore.

Miss Brebner, M.E.O., Malayan Nursing Service, General Hospital.

Miss Agnes Young, M.E.O., Malayan Nursing Service, General Hospital.

Miss Mabel Robinson, M.E.O., Malayan Nursing Service, General Hospital.

Miss M. Livingstone, M.E.O., Malayan Nursing Service, General Hospital.

Miss Anne Keir, M.E.O., Malayan Nursing Service, General Hospital.

Miss Lily Murray, M.E.O., Malayan Nursing Service, General Hospital.

Miss A. C. E. Myers, M.E.O., Malayan Nursing Service, General Hospital.

Miss May Wilde, M.E.O., Malayan Nursing Service, General Hospital.

Miss Mary Shehan, M.E.O., Malayan Nursing Service, General Hospital.

Miss Jean Milne, M.E.O., Malayan Nursing Service, General Hospital.

Miss M. Smith Woodyear, M.E.O., Malayan Nursing Service, General Hospital.

Miss M. J. Forgie, M.E.O., Malayan Nursing Service, General Hospital.

Miss Duncan and Mrs. Law (sisters), teachers, Penang.

Mrs. J. B. Ross, Mercantile Bank, Singapore. Miss Rayner, Teacher, Penang.

Mrs. Barnes, —

Mrs. Donald, Kuala Lumpur.

Mrs. O'Sullivan (Eve), Dress Shop, Singapore.

Miss Jessie Cameron, M.E.O.

Miss Annie Gibson, M.E.O.

Miss Jean Morrison, M.E.O.

Miss Eileen Try, M.E.O.

Miss E. McConnachy, M.E.O.

Mrs. Wright, husband with Commercial Union.

Mrs. Clarke, Penang Municipality.

Mrs. Esson, Bousteads.

Mrs. Jakeo, husband Planter, Perak.

Miss J. Thomson, M.E.O.

Miss J. D. Scott, M.E.O.

Miss De Ambrosie, M.E.O.

Miss M. Cork, M.E.O.

Mrs. Allen, husband Private Practitioner, Penang.

Mrs. Searer, husband Brigadier, R.A.M.C.

Mrs. Edwards, —

Nurse I. Theresa, —

Nurse Tan Choo Lim, —

Mrs. Roberston, husband A.P.C.

Dr. (Mrs.) Thompson, —

Miss Craig, sister of Dr. Craig, M.E.O., Education Department, Singapore.

[N.B. In the original 1943 text, the author added the following subtext: "The author would be grateful for any names or details which would make the above lists more complete. These could be sent to him c/o the publishers."]

∼

Government House, Singapore

c.1941

Read also :

ACROSS
MADAGASCAR

by

OLIVE MURRAY CHAPMAN

In this story of a journey across the great
island of Madagascar Mrs. Murray Chapman,
an investigator and explorer in the truest
sense of the word, reveals to us the mysteries
of life and death as they react on the minds of
the primitive natives ; she takes us across the
beautiful countryside, the great mountains,
the rivers and the lagoons, and she locks our
hearts and minds into the vast, mysterious,
primæval forests. The author travelled alone,
only occasionally accompanied by native
porters. Through the knowledge and history
of the country with which she infuses us and
the exciting adventures which the author encountered on her 2,000 3,000 mile journey
her account is one which will long live in
the memory. Some of the many original
photographs which Mrs. Murray Chapman
took are also reproduced in the book.

Illustrated. **9/6** *net.*

Ed. J. BURROW & Co., Ltd.

Cover Jacket of First Edition, 1943 (Back)

SINGAPORE
to
FREEDOM

The
vivid
record
of a
great
escape

by

OSWALD
W.
GILMOUR

With
23
Illustrations
and
a Map

BURROW

SINGAPORE
to
FREEDOM

by

OSWALD
W.
GILMOUR

With
23
Illustrations
and a Map

BURROW

This vivid and authentic story of the author's escape from Singapore just before the island fell describes his gruelling experiences in reaching the safety of Ceylon. A first-hand account, it illuminates an aspect of the Malayan tragedy which has yet to receive wide attention. Mr. Gilmour, who was Deputy Municipal Engineer of Singapore, has given us an absorbing narrative of the hazards and hardships of his experience. His book is not one easily to be abandoned.

10/6
NET

Cover Jacket of First Edition, 1943 (Front & Spine)

About the Author

Oswald Wellington Gilmour (1900 - 1978) was born in the town of Ballymena, Co. Antrim, Northern Ireland on the 3rd June 1900. Before the war, he worked in Singapore, and in 1940, he was given a command post in the Civil Defense Organization and was one of the last to leave the invaded city. After a series of adventures, he reached Ceylon, a journey described in this book (*Singapore to Freedom*).

Returning to England in 1942, he joined the Malaysian Planning Unit, set up by the War Office to plan for the re-occupation and received the rank of Colonel. By September, 1945, he was back in Singapore directing its engineering services. He stayed on for a time as Acting Municipal Engineer under civil government, writing about his experiences in a second book, *With Freedom to Singapore* (1950). He eventually returned to the United Kingdom to take up an engineering appointment on the constructional side of a large postwar town project.

Colonel Gilmour died in the town of Harlow, Essex, United Kingdom on the 19th August 1978.